THE NEW UNIVERSITY

CONTRIBUTORS

Adam Curle
W. Boyd Alexander
Wilfrid Harrison
W. H. G. Armytage
James Dundonald
Peter Karmel
W. H. Oliver

THE NEW
UNIVERSITY

Edited by
JOHN LAWLOR

New York
COLUMBIA UNIVERSITY PRESS

Published in 1968
by Columbia University Press
New York

© *John Lawlor 1968*

No part of this book may be reproduced
in any form without permission from
the publisher, except for the quotation
of brief passages in criticism

Library of Congress Catalogue Card Number: 68–8250

Printed in Great Britain
76290

Contents

Preface

These essays deal with certain problems and opportunities of university development in our time. The main focus is upon universities of the United Kingdom, but I have hoped to gain some advantages of perspective by including accounts of American and Commonwealth discussion and experiment. This is not to suggest for a moment that all the possibilities of change have been raised, let alone examined. The present collection can best be regarded as an informal interim report, where every speaker has had a free hand to deal with those problems or record those case-histories which he knows best from his own direct experience.

Mr. Curle's wide-ranging article sets a global scene, and draws some striking inferences from American practice. Dr. Alexander contributes a survey of the plans for English expansion as they struck an informed observer a year or two ago. I have not, save superficially, altered this record of one man's view of what seemed then in prospect, believing that the reader will profit most if he makes his own comparisons with the two articles which immediately follow. In the first, Professor Harrison describes some of the problems which were actually encountered, taking his own university as a leading instance; and in the second the account is brought fully up to date in Professor Armytage's 'Thoughts after Robbins'. Mr. Dundonald's contribution takes us a stage farther, into the possible stratification of existing universities and the prospects for any further development beyond present plans. Finally, in the two concluding chapters, Dr. Karmel presents an instructive case-history of one new development in Australia, and in a comprehensive survey Professor Oliver considers the relations between a society and its universities as illustrated in New Zealand.

The present book will succeed if it prompts others to revise their impressions of what is actual and their notions of what is possible in university development. As a first step towards that end, the publishers will be pleased to consider for publication contributions dealing with aspects of university development, primarily in the United Kingdom and Commonwealth, but by no means excluding American and other practice for comparison and contrast. Such contributions should be roughly equivalent in length to those appearing in the present book, and may be sent either to the publishers or directly to me.

University of Keele   JOHN LAWLOR
Staffordshire

UNIVERSITIES IN A CHANGING WORLD

Innovation and stagnation[1]

Adam Curle

Professor of Education and Development
Harvard University

[1] Based on a lecture given at the Danforth Foundation Workshop on Liberal Education, Colorado Springs, June 1966.

I look back on my own university days with a mixture of nostalgia and amazement. I am nostalgic because we had such a good time, because we were so little concerned with our education as a preparation for the world we were to enter, because it was a civilized and exciting sequel to the horrors of the secondary school. I look back with amazement because of the extraordinary insulation of the university which I attended from the realities of the world around us. I don't mean to say by this that no one took part in political activities, that no one was concerned about (for instance) the Spanish Civil War—but that the whole ambience of the place was to produce a civilized member of what was then still called the upper-classes in England, who was expected after a suitable period of preparation to go out and govern the colonies kindly but firmly, to administer the civil service which kept the elected politicians in control, to slaughter the king's enemies in vast quantities while writing poetry on the side, to preside over courts and sentence criminals to death, to run vast landed estates, to be a scholar and gentleman with equal emphasis on both roles. The idea that the university should in some way be geared to the exigencies of the time, should give heed to the demands of the economy, should in any sense question the supremacy of classical and other completely useless studies, was un-thinkable. Nobody worried very much whether we worked hard, but they would have worried exceptionally if we had not played hard. Admittedly the purpose of going to the university was to obtain an education; but the greater part of the education was something which was not gained from the things we learned, but from the friends we made and the urbane outlook and habit of life which we acquired.

(I)

All in all, during my youth, a considerable part of education in England was dedicated to preservation. And so it has been throughout the world. Until very recently, education has been the prerogative of the rulers and has served to establish and fortify in their children the traditional attitudes of the ruling group. It conserved the social system. It produced conformers rather than rebels. This does not mean that the old approach to the function of education did not produce men of brilliant and original abilities; but they were innovators only within a given framework.

Things began to change as more and more individuals and groups began to see that education could really alter things in a startling fashion. We are so used now to the idea that education creates opportunity that we forget how revolutionary the idea really is. Formerly it promoted the *status quo:* now it is perhaps the chief agent of social mobility. The change occurred at different times and at varying speeds in different parts of the world: in some it has not really taken place yet. In others, such as the U.S.A., it has dominated educational thinking for decades. (I should of course say, in passing, that education must have something of a conservative function as well; clearly, certain ideas and attitudes, a certain body of knowledge, have to be passed on. Paradoxically, society needs a certain stability of base from which to launch innovation. But there has been a very significant alteration of emphasis.)

The idea that education is a force making for change, that it gives the individual human being a tool to break the fetters of tradition and class structure, is linked to another. This is the concept of development, in the sense in which the word is used when we talk about developed or underdeveloped

4

nations. Of course the idea of economic growth in the wealthier countries of North America and Western Europe is not new, though of recent years we have become increasingly obsessed with the problem of maintaining growth rates. But for two-thirds of the world the idea is only twenty years old. In the developing areas of the world until about the end of the Second World War, the idea of growth was virtually unknown. The objective of most colonial rulers was to collect taxes and to maintain law and order. In India, for example, the officer in charge of a district was actually called a collector because of his prime task. Paradoxically, in independent India, now striving for development, he is still so named. This fact may indicate the survival of an attitude of mind which suggests why the strivings have reaped so little fruit. The colonial rulers, or some of them, really wanted something which was impossible. They hoped to improve conditions without altering the social system. They wished to go on ruling and did not want to create groups which might acquire the ambition to unseat them. So they aimed to preserve the *status quo*, but to make it more pleasant—to provide more and better social services, to educate in useful skills which would enable people to follow their traditional way of life with somewhat greater efficiency. It strikes some as strange that the same situation exists in countries which were not under colonial rule, such as those of Latin America, Afghanistan, Iran, Liberia and Ethiopia. Yet the reason is not far to seek, for these were ruled by oligarchies which, consisting of local people rather than transient imported administrators, had even more concern to keep the situation stable. But the surging political tides of the post-war era ensure that even in the most rigidly oligarchical societies such policies are hard to maintain. Everywhere—well, almost everywhere—the peoples of the world have their eyes focused on development. This does not mean simply an increase in *per capita* income, or even a rise in the standard of living, but a change in the social order, greater hope for the masses, more mobility for the individual. Education links these aspirations at two points. In the first place, it is to many peoples of the world a symbol of emancipation and hope. Secondly, it is thought of as something which actually promotes development. This second argument, very briefly, goes as follows. Developed countries need developed people to do things upon which development depends—to run the administration, to carry out the skilled tasks in industry, agriculture, and communications, and to teach the younger generation to do the same things. This concept must strike us as obvious, but economic theory for long suffered a strange blindness. Countries are poor, it stated, because they lacked capital: therefore what was needed was a financial loan or a gift, or at least help by supplying the machinery or technicians who would create the capital. But we would not apply the same standards to an individual. First we might well want to know why he was impoverished. Was it because he was an alcoholic or a gambler? Then he might need psychiatric treatment rather than a loan which would in a short time leave him no better off than he was. Was it because his lack of education made it hard to get good jobs? Then the first priority would be to get him into school. Was it because he spent all his substance on girls? Then what he needed most was a steady and economical wife. Now, happily, education is recognized as being, at least potentially, a powerful force in growth and change.

There is a third strand to the argument I am attempting to weave. This is the rate of technological development. The world is undergoing an incredible technical revolution, spearheaded by automation. There has been a great deal of scared talk about this. It will lead to massive unemployment; to a society in which there are only two hours work per person per week; to a society in which only ten per cent of the people are employed—and in this case what will happen to the American ethos of hard work rewarded by affluence?; to wide-spread alienation and political confusion; to brave new world or 1984—or the sort of benign concentration camp pictured by Jacques Ellul.

(II)

I tend to believe that these fears are grossly exaggerated but that they are based on potentialities inherent in some of the changes we are going through. We certainly need to take thought on how to exploit the extraordinary possibilities of our age, as well as to avoid its pitfalls. I would like to put forward two related propositions which I believe to be true.

The antidote to the problems generated by technology, is not less technology, but more of it. In order both to exploit and to avoid being overwhelmed by the newness and complexity of technological change, we need more and better education: we need people who are, in a sense, the antithesis of those who were produced by the traditional *status-quo*-preserving forms of education. We need people, firstly, who are free of facts, if I may speak extremely—who are able to think outside the context of gobbets of information and who rely rather on structure and theory to which information can be related. A few decades ago, the sciences we learned in youth were still valid in maturity. This is no longer so, and the techniques by which a man earns his living may alter so radically that in effect he has to learn five or six new jobs during his lifetime. This is so even in university teaching. Five successive generations of my family have taught in universities; but I am certain that my job-description would hardly be recognized by my uncles, still less so my grandfather. This means also that we live in several worlds undreamed of during the formative stages of our childhood, and that if we are to avoid the assault of *anomie* we must keep remarkably open and adaptable emotionally as well as intellectually. Add to that a creative and innovative spirit, and we have a formidable bundle of abilities for the universities to foster. So here are three new big things with which education is involved: social mobility for the individual, development for society, and the technological revolution. If the universities are to serve adequately in these three related spheres, they too will have to be as innovative, as unorthodox, as the purposes they should serve.

(III)

How then are the universities of the world meeting the challenge of the mid-twentieth century? Clearly any answer we can suggest must be highly impressionistic; but let us look at a few of the situations in the world today, taking first of all the sub-continent of India and Pakistan. The two countries together have a university and college population of about one and a half millions, of whom one and a quarter millions are in the sixteen hundred universities and colleges of India. This enrolment may not seem particularly high for so vast a country; but it is worth noting that it constitutes about the same proportion of the population as does the university population of the United Kingdom. Higher education in its present form in India and Pakistan derives from British rule. There had, of course, been the ancient seats of learning, Buddhist, Hindu, and Moslem, but the English rulers set a pattern which has survived and which has virtually obliterated all other sorts of institution. After much initial controversy the policies of Bentinck and Macaulay prevailed and British educational policy in the sub-continent was confirmed as being one whose great object should be, 'The promotion of European literature and science among the natives of India', and which should provide that 'all funds appropriated for the purposes of education would be employed on English education alone'. This of course implied that institutions were set up which had no roots in the cultural life of the country, which drew nothing from its scholarship and fields of medicine, rhetoric, astronomy, mathematics, philosophy, algebra, logic, grammar, and so on. Instead, students began to learn subject-matter which was not only entirely new but which was based on completely alien ways of thought and modes of looking at the world. It is impossible to avoid the feeling that this approach to university education is inevitably traumatic.

Nevertheless, whatever harm was done by the decision to divorce all higher learning from anything Indian was compounded by the fact that it was taught at a level much lower than that which prevailed in the model from which it was taken. This came about because of the structure of the university system in India. When it was decided to set up Indian universities (three were established in 1857), the government looked around for a model to follow. It was considered, and no doubt wisely, that Oxford and Cambridge were venerable and idiosyncratic institutions which could not readily be transplanted. The only other available models were the Scottish universities, which could hardly be thought appropriate since they *were* Scottish; the University of Durham, which was a sort of imitation of Oxford; and the University of London. The University of London consisted mainly of an administrative and examining organization which co-ordinated the work and set the standards for the group of colleges in London which had joined together in confederation. This seemed appropriate to India, since there were already a certain number of small colleges and since enough universities could not be started to cover the countryside as a whole. Consequently, each of the Indian universities had affiliated to it a number of colleges for which it set the syllabus and examinations. The University of Calcutta, for example, now has over 150 affiliated colleges. As the system has evolved, many of the colleges are far too small to maintain adequate academic standards. In fact the average size of the faculty of all institutions of higher education in India is under forty, whereas in the United States it is about 150. From their very inception Indian institutions of higher education have faced a problem of standards. Not only was there little or no surrounding culture to maintain an acceptable level in non-Indian studies, but there was no machinery for providing academic help from England. The unhappy students were not only cut off from their own culture but also from the sources of the alien culture that they were expected to absorb. It is small wonder that much academic work in the Indian universities acquired a kind of remote, brittle and artificial quality, a kind of ludicrous inappropriateness which has been the subject of many unkind jokes and which sadly inhibited the universities' capacity to contribute to national development. This is not to say, of course, that no attempts were made to keep the standards high—of course there were —but the whole environment was against them. Moreover, by one of the unhappy paradoxes which haunt the process of development, the very measures set up to improve quality were some of those which were most effectively instrumental in depressing it. The main role of the central universities was to maintain the standards of the affiliated colleges. This was done chiefly through the examination system. But where the general examination is set by an external body there is apt to be an impersonality and almost an obtuseness about the whole arrangement. Inevitably, moreover, the whole work of the college becomes directed towards the passing of the examination and not towards the acquiring of scholarship. Those who have taught in the colleges of India and Pakistan—where the system was just the same—have found that on the whole teachers have taught only the basic minimum of what was required by the syllabus and have substituted cramming for education. Students have been quick to rebuke teachers who have wandered, often for the sake of interesting or illuminating example, from the text-book, and have seldom acquired any of the interest and excitement of learning.

But then we must ask why the examinations are so important. The acquisition of a degree has come, particularly in the former colonial countries, to be a passport into the realm of affairs in which real power is wielded. In Asia, as in Africa, young men strive to enter the service of the government because for so long this was the only sphere in which they could emulate the authority of their rulers—and for this a B.A. degree was essential. For the same reason, other types of education have been rejected. In the colonial days many well-meaning administrators sought to promote agricultural and technical education, only to find that this was bitterly resented as an attempt to keep the native peoples in their position of subservience, to fob them off with something second-best and prevent them from sharing in, and perhaps eventually usurping, the white man's power. Consequently today the universities of India, and indeed of many other Asian countries, spew out tens of thousands of students with degrees in such subjects as law, the humanities, and social science, because, although there are no jobs to be obtained in these fields, they are thought of as constituting entry to the positions in society which carry the most prestige. Let me just observe that in the universities of the Philippines in 1960 there were 102,000 students in the social sciences; 11,000 in law; 4,000 in agriculture; and 2,000 in natural science.

In the context of our reference to technical development it is perhaps significant that in India at the same time slightly less than five per cent of the total enrolment in higher education is in schools of engineering. In Poland the figure is thirty per cent. In the U.S.S.R., out of three million students in higher education just over half are in science, engineering and agriculture.

(IV)

Although the Indian universities ought to provide an object-lesson in how not to educate, the system has at least been in existence for a hundred years and is, for better or for worse, well established. In British tropical Africa, however, there was, except for one sickly institution, no higher education whatsoever until a quarter of a century ago. During the Second World War, however, the British began to think in terms of educating the African peoples to take over the control of their destinies, and began to set up institutions of higher education throughout their dependencies. Some of these were entirely new, as the universities and colleges in Ghana, Nigeria and Rhodesia: others were grafted on to existing institutions of lower calibre in the Sudan, Uganda, etc. In almost all respects the approach was entirely different from what had been applied in India, and consciously so, for the British authorities were uneasily aware of the disasters which had overtaken Indian education because of the errors of judgement of their predecessors. But by no means all of the Indian mistakes were rectified, and others were made in the very attempt at reform.

The greatest efforts were made to ensure that the academic standards remained high. This was done by placing the new 'university colleges'—for such was the name given in the British system to institutions of higher education which did not award their own degrees—under the academic tutelage of London University. This meant that the entry standards were established by London and that the examinations were jointly set and jointly examined by the faculties of the college concerned both in Africa and in London University. This special relationship, as it is termed, proved extraordinarily effective in the production of scholars of high quality. But the fact that these colleges were academically modelled to a large extent upon London meant that the content and the character of the syllabus was British-oriented, and in consequence that much was left undone which might have helped students to understand their own country's problems, to adjust to the needs of developing nations, and to apply western science to the problems of Africa. An equally serious criticism was that by limiting the intake of students to those who had reached an acceptable British standard, the portals of higher education were opened initially to an extraordinarily small number of Africans; whereas what was needed most by the continent at that time was a flood of vigorous young people who had had their minds awakened and their horizons widened, but who were not necessarily meticulous academics. The situation in Africa led to some absurdities. Even in 1965, when I was in Nigeria, I discovered that a practice I had first known some eight or nine years ago and had considered certainly defunct after the independence of the West African countries, was still in existence. This entailed sending over from England ordinary English country flowers packed carefully in ice to be dissected during botany practical examinations in the schools. This might at one stage have been considered a kind of floral chauvinism of the colonial rulers; and that it should go on after the independence of Nigeria struck me as bizarre. I was told, however, that no sufficiently systematic study of Nigerian fauna or flora had yet been carried out and that reliance still had to be placed on flowers which had been extensively studied. The same sort of arguments might be used for the prominence of English geography and history in the Nigerian textbooks—these subjects have simply not been adequately studied in relation to Africa as yet. I would add that work to rectify this terrible lack is going on all over the place and has already led to some significant contributions to scholarship; but there is a considerable contrast with India where the tradition of Indian scholarship and learning stretches back unbroken for hundreds of years. The colonial educators did not have much African material to use; but they certainly ignored the riches that India had to provide.

It is an interesting fact that the greatest reform of African higher education has come from the New World. The former president of Nigeria, Dr. Azikiwe, sponsored the establishment of the University of Nigeria at Nsukka. This was supported by United States A.I.D.[1] and, working with an A.I.D. contract, Michigan State University. This was a bold move to introduce the land-grant[2] principle into Nigeria; and so far as can be told it has worked surprisingly well. To start with, the conditions of entry were markedly relaxed; and this is clearly a sensible thing when standards of schooling vary so much that to rely on the criterion of academic performance seems very likely to exclude numbers of potentially good people. Next, the more pragmatic, service-oriented, approach of the university fitted both the needs and the mood of Africa. Thirdly, so far as we can tell,

[1] Agency for International Development. In President Johnson's 1966–7 Budget submission to Congress (24 January 1966), expenditure under this programme was estimated as rising from $2,041 million in 1964–5 to $2,100 million in 1965–6 and $2,200 million in 1966–7. [Ed.]

[2] The Land-Grant College Act (1862) was the essential step in the development of a system of state educational institutions aided by the federal government. The bill (originally introduced in 1857) donated 'public lands to the several States and Territories which may provide colleges for the benefit of agriculture and the mechanic arts' (*Cong. Globe*, 35 Cong., I Sess., p. 32). [Ed.]

the actual results being achieved by scholars trained in Nsukka are in no sense inferior to those of the more Oxbridge-oriented alumni of the university of Ibadan. The universities of Africa are still in a state of flux. It is hard to tell what shape they will take in the future; but the model of Nsukka seems at the moment to be the most propitious.

(V)

To move from Asia and Africa to Latin America does not so much take us across the Atlantic as back in time to the medieval splendours of Bologna and Salamanca. Many of the Latin American universities are extremely old. One in Santo Domingo was founded about a hundred years before Harvard but has, as far as I can judge, been getting steadily worse ever since it was established. Although there are of course some exceptions, the universities of Latin America have developed in remarkably similar ways. Almost all, for example, glorify the student through the principle of 'co-gobierno', the principle which allows students a place, even in some cases a majority, on every committee of any importance within the university. At the same time, however, they leave them almost entirely devoid of adequate scholastic help, or of social or political guidance. Students have all too much power in the politics of their countries and their universities, but very little constructive thought is given to shaping either national or academic policies. Noisy street battles involving what are virtually professional students dominate the political scene, but do not promote sound scholarship. The universities in fact, through the second principle of 'autonomía', have very little contact with the countries to which they owe their support. Although depending upon the government for their revenues they resist any attempt to serve their nations in any practical way: to do so would be an affront to their autonomy. In this spirit they scorn cultures where the sciences are applied with vigour, yet their concerns about their own short-comings in this respect have led to a decay of the more academic studies in which they claim to glory. They despise the empiricism of American universities, claiming that their scholarship is debased by their practicality. They extol such abstract studies as philosophy, pure science, political theory, but without developing the methodologies needed for their studies, or applying them practically in the arena of life. Archaic, proud, isolated, the universities of Latin America are in decay, their professors ill-paid, holding—some of them—three or four university appointments simultaneously as well as an outside position.

And how are we doing in the western world? Here of course the scene is much more complex, the diversity much greater. It is very hard to give any general impressions that can have the slightest validity. I might, however, mention British education. British university education appears to me to be affected still by what I believe to be a widespread characteristic of British society. It is still very exclusive. Whereas in the United States about one citizen in every thirty is enrolled in some form or other of higher education, the proportion in England is only one in every two hundred. Higher education is, in fact, still thought of by many as the prerogative of a small number of the *élite*. The universities have in general also maintained a far greater separation from the world of affairs than have those of the United States. (I would emphasize that I am speaking here of the best universities of the United States: there is far less difference between the best and the worst of the English system than there is among the two thousand-odd American degree-giving institutions. The great majority of the British universities would probably rank somewhere among the top twenty-five per cent of the American colleges and universities; and it is with these that I would compare them.) There are probably two reasons for this. The first is the fact that in affluent America the worlds of government, commerce and industry have recognized the value of the universities and draw heavily upon their resources at the same time as they contribute to the development of those resources through a wide variety of grants and foundations.

The second reason is simply the traditional isolation of the academic from the world in which he lives.

(VI)

So much, for the time being, for the universities. What about the world in which education can play such a tremendous part? On one side enormous progress is being made. The colonial era is virtually over and for millions there would appear to be opportunities of growth and change incomparably better than anything which had existed beforehand. Many of the killing epidemics have been brought under control—yellow fever, bubonic plague, smallpox and cholera no longer bring their trail of disaster. Improvement in communication and the spread of literacy have brought the peoples of the world into contact with—or at least to have some knowledge of—each other, as never before. Perhaps the best thing of all is that the nations of the world, for the first time in history, are prepared in a spirit of altruism —albeit tinged with political realism—to help each other.

But these good things have brought concomitant dangers, quite apart from the perils of modern warfare, which obviously spring from our technological advances. Improvements in public health have led to a dangerous expansion of the world's population: improvements in communication have led to jealousies and resentments which constantly imperil the precarious balance of world affairs. The rejection of colonialism has led to a heightening and expansion of racial tension and intolerance. The very aid which is given creates friction which had not existed before. And how useful in fact is the aid? The United States, which nobly pioneered the efforts of the rich to help the poor, has reduced a proportion of national income spent on non-military assistance from two to less than one half per cent per annum of gross national product. Some of the citizens of the under-developed areas are very cynical about foreign assistance. They note that the rich countries in fact reserve all their trade for each other. Indeed, more and more do the wealthier nations constitute a self-sufficient and very prosperous block who neither need nor make great sacrifices to help their poorer brethren—who, in consequence, fall farther and farther behind. As the gap between the rich and the poor grows wider, however, we try to assuage the helpless resentment of our less fortunate fellow human beings by a great display of rather inexpensive generosity. Or so it seems to some of them.

Perhaps the most significant new development in today's world is that it is self-conscious. It knows what it wants and it envies those who have it—enough food, reasonable medical facilities, enough resources to escape from the grinding misery of absolute poverty; and it knows that it is infinitely far from achieving these things. I must emphasize how incredibly hard it is for a country with nothing to achieve anything. Take Ethiopia, for example. When I was there in 1959 there were for about fifteen million people fourteen Ethiopian doctors. This ratio of one doctor to every million inhabitants is to be compared with one doctor to every 760 in the United States! How does one *begin*, even assuming one has enough money to build a health service on so microscopic a base? How does one use the fourteen doctors not only to serve the needs of a gigantic country but also to train new physicians and nurses? The logistics of such an operation appal one. I hasten to point out that the medical situation in Ethiopia is not quite as bad as these figures suggest. There are a number of foreign doctors there and the number has greatly increased since the time of which I speak. This importation of foreigners perhaps makes some kind of logistical expansion possible. But if all the under-developed countries of the world were to receive the assistance they really required, not only to build up their health services but educational systems and techniques of developing their resources, then the developed areas would themselves be suffering crippling shortages. The stark fact is that there are just not enough trained people to go around. Even the highly educated countries, such as the United States, the countries of western Europe, and the U.S.S.R., are not producing them quickly enough; while the countries

17

of the underdeveloped world are falling very seriously behind, partly because their skilled men flock over here. It is hard to see how and when the supply of trained people—and I do not mean the unemployed humanists and legal experts of India—will ever catch up with, let alone overtake, the burgeoning demand; and the demand has to burgeon if the urgent needs are to be met.

All in all, although there has been progress in some places, growth has been slow and disappointing—except, of course, the growth of population, and this is half the trouble. It is reckoned that unless things become appreciably better, by the year 2000 the population which is hungry, unnecessarily sick from chronic diseases which are much harder to eradicate than the quick killers, which is poor, illiterate and in general disadvantaged, will have grown from two thirds to four fifths of the whole. From every point of view, this is a sombre prospect. The extraordinary degree of affluence in which we live in the United States (or at least in which four fifths of us live) should never blind us to the miseries of so many of our brothers, or of the danger for us of these miseries. In fact, if we think back for a moment to the three interrelated issues, whose importance for the educator I stressed—mobility for the individual, development for society, and technological growth—we see that they are more potent in promise than in performance. We have also to acknowledge that, at least in the areas we looked at, the contribution of the universities is much less than might have been hoped. It is true that the technology exists, but it has not been diffused: the ideas of equality and mobility are widespread and powerful, but unless they can lead to social change and a widening of individual opportunity, they turn sour; development is recognized as a great goal, but it is atrociously hard to get pauper economies off the ground before ballooning populations eat up all their hard-won gains.

(VII)

Although the word innovation appears in the title of this

chapter I have said virtually nothing about it. I have dwelt on continuing traditions of education, on attitudes towards learning in academic institutions translated from bygone eras into the twentieth century, when flexibility is needed most of all. There has been all too little innovation to talk about. Had there been, this story might have been different. But let us now try to think of the sort of approach to the task of the university which might conceivably contribute more actively to the issues we are considering.

I take it first of all that any education which is to realize the aroused hopes of an individual, to give him the capacity to move freely in society rather than in the thrall of its class-structure, must be generally available. That is surely axiomatic. But at once we encounter formidable obstacles. On the educational side we meet those who assert, and not without evidence, that the proportion of students who can profit from the high level of education is relatively small. We come up against the old Jacksonian-Jeffersonian dichotomy of concentration on the *élite* or spreading very thinly the jam of culture.

On the economic side we come against a set of rather involved arguments. On the one hand we are told that even if a country can afford to expand its university structure up to a certain point it will merely be creating unemployment. Poor countries are poor in job-opportunities, and it is easier to produce graduates, particularly from lower levels of education, than to make jobs for them. The primary school leaver who haunts the towns of West Africa hoping for employment which would have been readily available to his father in a less literate age is a national liability, both politically and economically. But there is another side to this argument. To gear educational expansion to projections of economic growth and consequently to job-creation is to treat the economy as though it were a prime mover in its own growth, and to assume that this is something which occurred without human agency. But we know, of course, that it is the energy, initiative, innovative capacity, and entrepreneurial talent of individual human beings which brings development about. This being so, we would limit possible economic expansion if we were to adjust the output of students to carefully projected needs for trained personnel. Some people would certainly like to do this; but luckily it is very hard to do—the French tried and failed, and now are very glad that they did fail, because at the time when they made their projections the development of automated processes had not been predicted. This would argue against the limitation, on economic grounds, of educational growth. A related argument would stress the imponderable advantage to society as a whole of competent and alert citizens. The key to decision here is, perhaps, not so much numbers but the field in which people have been educated and the quality they have achieved. And this brings us back to the educational arguments and the Jacksonian-Jeffersonian antithesis.

Our educational system has not demonstrated that it is possible *both* to cultivate the able *and* to raise the level of the mediocre. But it is conceivable that this is because our concept of excellence has been narrow. It is undoubtedly true that the number of children who can achieve outstanding results in schools is limited. But our concept of outstanding results is also limited. It is not even very realistic. We assume, I suppose, that good results in school are important because they are predictive of high achievement in later life. It is indeed hard to consider that there could be any other criterion. But are they really? Studies carried out of the career-pattern of scientists in England show that those who went on to achieve high honours in their field were no better at undergraduate level than those who did not. Analysis of the academic record of scientists such as Einstein and Darwin suggests that had these applied for grants for graduate study today they would probably have been denied. A great deal of evidence on this type of point suggests that the net with which we fish for abilities in school has a wide mesh through which escape many of the qualities which really indicate promise. All that we are left with is the ability of a child to play the conventional game as the school demands it—to write essays, to answer questions, to pass tests, and so on. I am not saying that this ability is definitely antipathetic to subsequent high achievement; it may indeed indicate a high and adaptable ability on the part of the student who can adjust himself to the needs of the system. But it would seem that the qualities which really go to make for high performance are such things as creativeness, imagination, perseverance, concentration, energy, interest, determination, leadership, the psychological need for achievement, and other things which school-systems neither recognize in their tests of performance nor attempt in any systematic fashion to instil. Indeed one is sometimes left with the unfortunate fear that our schools are suspicious of such qualities as originality. Getzels and Jackson, for example, find that teachers preferred children with high I.Q.s to those with highly creative minds. One reason was that the high I.Q. students were prepared to accept the *mores* and standards of the school, while those they term the high creatives—who suffered in consequence—were not.

They tell an entertaining story illustrating this fact. Children are shown a series of cards and asked to write stories accounting for action displayed on the cards. One was of a man sitting in an aeroplane smiling broadly to himself. The interpretation which gained high praise from the teacher was to the general effect that he was a salesman returning from a successful business tour. He was sitting back anticipating the pleasure of buying his wife a new mink coat and taking her out to dine at the country club. They were going to consume, of course, steak, ice cream, and martinis. The child who got low marks and was indeed reprobated for his tastelessly anti-social interpretation said that on the contrary he saw the man in the picture as returning from Reno where he had just divorced his wife. He divorced her because she put so much face-cream on her face at night that her head kept sliding across the pillow and knocking into him. He told the judge that he could not sleep because of this. An additional reason why he was smiling was because he had just made up a formula for anti-skid face-cream out of which he hoped to make a fortune.

Our educational system is also such that to all intents and purposes it denies the existence of certain sorts of talent. Creative talent in the arts, for example, receives scant recognition, while technical education has always been treated as a sort of poor step-sister. In this connection the Harvard Report on general education in a free society commented that 'it is a strange state of affairs in an industrial democracy where those very subjects are held in disrepute which are at the heart of the national economy and those students by implication condemned who will become its operators'. It is a strange irony that what we call general education in fact excludes a major part of what would make it most general and most universal in the modern world. These considerations lead me to advocate a policy which might be termed 'equal opportunity for diversity of talent'. But I do not merely mean that we should attempt to promote and develop ability of every sort rather than murdering one ability by attempting to turn it into another. I mean that if we understand the process of human development properly we will find that there are many ways to excellence, even academic excellence. The child who is good with his hands, as we say, at one stage is not necessarily the one who lacks formal academic promise at a later stage; but his route towards scholarship may be through developing his manipulative skills. The same might be said about other forms of ability. Our problem, it seems to me, is to change our criteria of excellence and to devise an educational system which will not only admit to the existence of many types of excellence but which will also identify and encourage the other qualities which lead to high achievement. I will not attempt to say what this might mean for the structure of our universities; but clearly it would involve innovations of a major order.

(VIII)

There are two other fields of change. The first, at which I

have already hinted, refers less to subject-matter than to the ways in which subject-matter is taught. The type of learning exemplified by the new mathematics, which is based on an attempt to impart the principles of structure, undoubtedly gives us the raw intellectual capacity to deal with situations unthought of at the time when we received our instruction. It is particularly important, although much more difficult, that this type of appreciation should be applied to work in the field of the social studies, thus giving us some means of threading our way through the mazes of the world yet unborn. One other field in which I believe much innovation needs to be carried out is in the technique of policy-formation for education. In a country in which the bulk of education is carried out either by private institutions of higher education or separate school systems, the chance of planning and systematizing educational policy is infinitely difficult; and although there are undoubted advantages in diversity there are equally undoubted ills in failures of collaboration. At this juncture of history, particularly if the universities are to play their most effective part in the development of the technical society, it would seem a matter of most urgency that the universities—the producers of skilled labour—should learn how to work with the industries—the consumers of that labour. Some form of integrated planning, and even of collaboration in training, may prove one of the most fruitful links between the world of academia and that of the market-place.

I hope it will be appreciated that during the last few pages much of what I have said could be applied to, even if it was not directly aimed at, the American colleges and universities. But I have hoped that what I have had to say about other institutions would have some bearing on them. After all, the problems of preparing young people to live effectively, creatively, and—with luck—happily, have much in common wherever we live. And although the immediate contexts differ, we know that we live in the same world, a world in which whatever happens anywhere affects us all. We are all, indeed, members of one another. So I hope that these rambling reflections on problems and places with which I have been personally concerned will not impede any one group in focusing attention on its own districtive concerns.

Let me end, however, with an observation on a quality of higher education which, if not exclusively American, is at least to be seen in the United States in its fullest development. I refer to the involvement in the world of affairs which I mentioned briefly a little earlier. This, it seems to me, marks a turning-point in the evolution of higher education. The ivory tower and the absent-minded professor are no longer things people even bother to joke about. The professor is now a part of the world in which he lives. He does his stint with government, he becomes an ambassador, he advises industry and government on a score of vital matters. He may even go too far, forgetting that he has any students; but for most teachers and colleges this interplay with the real world is of inestimable value. It contributes enormously to scholarship and teaching, for the man who can test his knowledge against the harsh situations he encounters outside the cloister, gains knowledge. He gains knowledge and perspective which in turn, when he comes back, enrich his scholarship.

All this means I believe, that the college is becoming a new sort of institution. Certainly it is one greatly respected in the rest of the world and various studies tell us that the most honoured professions now are those of the professor and the physician. But more important, it is becoming a centre of interplay for the worlds of ideas and action. There is a new kind of openness about it. Indeed the word 'cloister' which I used just now is hardly appropriate. There is a new striving and energy, drawing from and fusing both the academic traditions and the realities of government, business, industry and international relations. It is out of this fusion that there is emerging, I believe, and will increasingly emerge, the capacity for change and innovation which will enable our colleges, and eventually the colleges of the world, to fulfil their highest purpose.

ENGLAND'S NEW SEVEN
An American view[1]

W. Boyd Alexander
Dean of the Faculty, Emeritus
Antioch College, Ohio

[1] Based on the Antioch College Faculty Lecture for 1965, presented in Dayton, Ohio, 5 March 1965.

C

(I)

As a student of higher education long interested in the English origins of our American colleges, I have visited English universities and their constituent colleges upon several occasions. I should add that our universities were built on German models beginning less than 100 years ago with Johns Hopkins.

My first visits were in 1950 when the first substantial number of Antioch students studied for a year in English universities. That was six years before the Antioch Education Abroad programme was formally launched. There were four students at Bristol and at Exeter (then under the aegis of the University of London), one at North Staffordshire, which later became the University of Keele, one at Ruskin College at Oxford, and one at University College, London. On sabbatical leave that year I visited at their respective institutions and met them all again several times in Paris at the Christmas holiday. A colleague spending a year at Bristol reported that he was assigned a seminar on the American revolution. Upon my inquiry as to what other courses were given in American history, he replied—just one, a general survey taught by a young Oxford M.A. who had never been to the U.S.A. This humbling fact reminded me of our colonial unimportance, on the periphery of the English cultural world. Later I believe my colleague helped the young teacher to take a Ph.D. in American history at Yale.

Four times since then I have made brief forays into the

English academic territory without casualty and with an increase each time in my respect and appreciation for the high standards of the English universities. Though five English universities were founded[1] between World War II and 1960, only one, Keele, differed in basic philosophy, curriculum, and method from the standard civic model.

By American standards the number of university students in England is small in both absolute and comparative terms. There were only 140,000 in 1964, including 19,000 at the ancient universities of Oxford and Cambridge. Counting in the colleges of advanced technology and the colleges of education and others, the total was about 230,000. There were over $4\frac{1}{2}$ million in American universities and colleges and well over 2 million in the junior year and above. Making allowance for the difference in total population, our percentage of students in higher education was $2\frac{1}{2}$ to 5 times as much as England's.

In the later 1950s the University Grants Committee (U.G.C.), a non-partisan agency of Parliament, including eminent academicians, authorized the creation of seven new universities in England. They departed from custom by authorizing them to grant their own degrees from the beginning rather than to 'earn their passage' by a long tutelage under an existing university. The University of London had fathered the fourteen Redbrick city universities by its external degree system, which is still in use. Last year (1963-4) the university, which administers its examinations in other Commonwealth countries as well as in England, had 25,000 'external' students, almost as many as 'internal' students at London.

Localities were invited to apply for a new university to be placed in a spacious campus nearby, though 'bid' might be a more appropriate term than 'apply'. The U.G.C. offered to give major support to the new universities for academic buildings and operating expenses but expected

---

[1] The writer is obviously including in this total those former university colleges which were accorded university status in the period under review. [Ed.]

the locality to provide the land and a generous amount of capital. While the new universities were to be partly residential and to have that flavour, the U.G.C., it turned out, would make no grants for residence halls. Sponsoring boards of prominent people were organized to attempt to capture the new universities and to secure land and raise money for them, because they were viewed as economic as well as cultural assets to successful communities. Distinguished academic planning boards were appointed and given great latitude by the U.G.C. in all aspects of planning. It was generally agreed that the new institutions were commissioned to pioneer, and to use the Oxbridge and Redbrick traditions and examples only to the extent they chose. Sussex, the first new institution to be accorded the title of university even before it had opened its doors to students, received its Royal Charter in 1961. The city of Brighton, the famous seaside resort where George IV built his oriental pleasure palace, had long hoped for a university to enrich its culture and commerce. A university project begun in 1911 had been brought to an end by World War I. In 1956 the Brighton City Council adopted proposals that led to the Royal Charter of 1961.

From various sources I learned that the new universities were making bold and exciting plans and that some of their curricular ideas were new and challenging. When I was elected to give the Faculty Lecture I decided to make a study of them and to visit several of them in October, 1964, on my way home from Paris. I believed that some account of their new ideas and plans might interest the Antioch faculty and that some of the new ideas might have applications or adaptations here.

My schedule permitted me to visit only two of the new institutions—the University of Sussex at Brighton and the University of Essex at Colchester. In each place I was fortunate enough to know a prominent faculty member who served as my guide and mentor, and to meet the Vice-Chancellor briefly. Sussex, now in its fourth year, was well established on an old estate three and a half miles east of

Brighton, with 1,600 students, over 200 faculty, and several new buildings in an architectural style that reminded me of Eero Saarinen's. For example, there were reflecting pools where one might have expected gardens and there was a free and original use of brick, concrete, and glass.

Essex, about as far north of London as Brighton is to the south, a little over fifty miles, was in its first year and the new buildings were just coming out of the ground. It was using the old manor house and some Nissen huts for its hundred or so students and proportionately larger faculty. Here Professor R. G. Lipsey was my helpful host.

I have used several books, articles, and university documents as bases for this study. One of them was the Robbins Report of the Committee on Higher Education, appointed by the Prime Minister, which laboured for two years, 1961–63, under the chairmanship of Lord Robbins, to bring out its report and recommendations, some of which have already been acted upon. For example, the committee recommended that the ten colleges of advanced technology should all be given university status. This has been accomplished so that they can now grant degrees rather than only certificates and diplomas as heretofore. Another very helpful book was *The Idea of a New University: An Experiment in Sussex* (1964), edited by David Daiches, who is Dean of the School of English and American Studies at Sussex. He was the man I knew there. Yet another was *A University in the Making* (1964), by Albert E. Sloman, the Vice-Chancellor of the University of Essex. Also, I have consulted the prospectuses of Sussex, Essex, York, and Keele, as well as numerous newspaper articles including one by Pendennis in the *Observer* of 14 June 1964, entitled 'The Seven Brave Young Britains.'

(II)

Now I shall take a few steps backward in British history to establish the social, economic, and political context into which the 'seven brave young Britains' are so boldly stepping. Just over fifty years ago the British Empire was the world's greatest power. The Pax Britannica had lasted for the century since Waterloo. The Boer War at the turn of the century and the blustering build-up of the German Empire produced cracks in the structure. But in 1914 the little off-shore European island ruled one quarter of the globe and dominated the rest of it by virtue of its naval, political, economic, and cultural power. Half a century and two world wars later, in both of which Britain organized winning coalitions, the Empire is almost all gone, though most of it remains in the loose federation of the Commonwealth. In these wars Britain sacrificed the flower of her youth and expended untold treasure that had been accumulating for centuries. Now the United Kingdom, of which England is the major part, though it still has much 'invisible income' from its long established commercial ventures, has few natural resources left. With a large population used to a high standard of living on a small island, it must live by its wits—that is by selling its technological, business, and even its cultural services to the rest of the world.

All the attributes of Britain's former glory have been lost or greatly reduced except, paradoxically, her cultural ascendancy. She has lost an empire but gained a world. Her cultural realm grows apace as the English language becomes more and more the lingua franca of international affairs, world trade, science, and the other academic fields. This is Britain's greatest remaining asset from her two centuries of empire. But she must exploit and develop it or it may shrink, too, in the fierce international competition of the last third of this century.

Professor Fritz Machlup of Princeton University has attempted recently in his book, *The Production and Distribution of Knowledge in the United States*,[1] to estimate the size and scope of the knowledge-industry. He includes in his definition of knowledge every kind of information, however generated or communicated. His thesis is that knowledge is the modern world's most important product. He counts

[1] See an interesting review in *Fortune*, November 1964.

not only the schools, colleges and universities, but all other propagation of knowledge by business and industry, by research, by publishing, by radio and TV, by the government, and other factors one might easily miss.

Dr. Machlup puts the output of our knowledge-industry as about one-third of our gross national product and shows that it is growing faster each year than the total economy. As the knowledge-industry grows it stimulates the rest of the economy to grow and then grows further and faster itself on the increased social production. Research and development is the fastest growing sector of the knowledge industry. Of course it is dependent on the educational system to produce its personnel.

It is in the knowledge-sector of world production that the British have the greatest advantage in world competition. Powerful as the United States may be it is, after all, merely a hitch-hiker in England's culture car. Of course, the British must use their manufacturing and trading skills to the full; but because they have to buy their raw materials before they can sell them back to the rest of the world they are at an increasing disadvantage as almost every nation tries to foster industry of its own. Their research men are still among the best in the world and so are their facilities for producing them—that is, their universities. However, they are too few in number. The United States carries on a major part of the pure research of the world and does some of it with British scientists brought here by the 'brain drain'. These leading scientists are attracted to the United States not so much by higher salaries as by our enormous and rapidly growing facilities for research in libraries and in large and expensive equipment. The Robbins Report points out that in 1960 the University of California alone spent four-fifths as much on libraries as did all the British universities combined. Britain's big problem in the university field is to maintain a critical mass—that is, to develop its universities and its research faster rather than slower than the rest of the world. Another paradox here is that the United States, Britain's firmest ally, is its greatest rival in university development and the production of scholars, knowledge, and research.

Many people in Britain realized in the 1950s that it was falling behind in the academic procession at the same time that its share of world trade was decreasing. The University Grants Committee authorized the seven new universities. Getting born as a university takes a long time. Sussex got going first in 1961 because of Brighton's long-standing ambitions, but it was 1963 before East Anglia, at Norwich, and York got under way, and 1964 before Essex and Lancaster admitted their first students. Kent at Canterbury and Warwick at Coventry will open this year. All of them are starting very small. They plan to grow rapidly but only to sizes—5,000 to 10,000 by 1980—that we should consider modest. However, this is considered policy. Enormous universities like some of ours are not wanted because the U.G.C. evidently believes that large size brings with it insuperable educational and social problems.

The U.G.C. laid down the following eight basic principles:

1 That the new universities would have degree-granting powers from the outset;

2 That they would be built on spacious campuses, outside cities, and be residential to a large degree;

3 That they would have three-year undergraduate curricula like Oxbridge and the Redbricks, which was a decision against following the experimental four-year example of the University of Keele;

4 That they would be organized around schools of related subjects with a broader curriculum than the old universities, where the student came straight from the sixth form of his grammar school into deep and intensive specialization in a single subject or discipline. Again rejected was the example of Keele, which had set up a first year of general education with the student required to take broad courses in both science and the humanities. Keele, founded in 1949, had undertaken a programme to protect 'the student's right to become a capable and

cultivated human being from the insistent demands of specialism and vocationalism'. But its programme had proved expensive with its extra year and a low faculty-student ratio and in 1963 it still had only 813 students.[1]

5 The U.G.C. announced that it would support the new universities within its financial power, which meant to the extent Parliament would grant the needed funds, by both capital and operating grants, but that it would expect local initiative to share generously in both.

6 Despite the intention that the new universities should be residential to a large extent, the U.G.C. decided eventually not to make grants to build or subsidize the operation of halls of residence.

7 Graduate work was to be undertaken almost from the beginning and research of all sorts was to be encouraged and developed as rapidly as possible. The U.G.C. believed that good university teaching could take place only in an atmosphere of research and creativity. The new universities were to put new and greater stress on teaching and on the university as a community for personal growth, but they were to give great weight to research also—that is, they were to be teaching-research universities with each factor in the equation supporting the other.

8 The new universities were to enrich the culture and contribute in appropriate ways to the industry and commerce of their cities and their neighbourhoods.

Whether the U.G.C. made these principles entirely specific or even promulgated them in an official document, I am not certain, but they all seem to have been used as guidelines in varying degrees by the seven new universities.

The seven new universities, even if they all grow to 3,000 enrolment by 1970, will make only a small dent in the number needed. The Robbins Report states that in 1963 there were 216,000 students in all phases of higher educa-

---

[1] It should be observed that Keele's numbers were designedly low. An essential aspect of the full university education envisaged by Keele's first Principal, Lord Lindsay of Birker, was a small undergraduate population, originally set at a total of 600. [Ed.]

tion. Only a little over half of these, 130,000, were in the universities. It predicts a need for 350,000 places in higher education by 1970, 219,000 in universities, and 560,000 places by 1980, 350,000 in universities. The other 210,000 places for 1980 would be 145,000 in colleges of education for training teachers and 65,000 in various other kinds of 'further' education—for example, schools of art.

All of these figures seem to me underestimates in terms of Britain's need and even in terms of the committee's own criterion that higher education should be available to all qualified school-leavers. Surprisingly, the committee did not attempt even an educated guess at what effect the changing patterns of occupations might have on its long-range plans. Inevitably, I think, the growth of the knowledge-industry and the reduction in manual workers that automation will bring about will require an increasing proportion of better educated and trained workers. For this reason I fear that the Robbins Committee has underestimated the long-term needs.

Miss Gwen Gardner of our Antioch Education Abroad staff, to whom I am indebted for valuable help on this paper, has brought back dramatic and discouraging news about the British government's plans for university development. Last week[1] the government announced that no new universities will be authorized in the next ten years. This decision must reflect serious weakness in the British financial situation because it was made in the face of the Robbins Report's recommendation that six more new universities should be started immediately to provide for 30,000 more students by 1980.

The term 'qualified school-leavers' means sixth-form graduates. The English school system needs to produce many more of them to feed the universities. The Robbins Report makes much of the small percentage of wastage (of those who enter the English universities) compared to other countries, especially the United States. While it gives the facts that show a tremendous wastage of potential university

[1] i.e. late February, 1965. [Ed.]

35

students who never get there because of social and cultural disadvantages and the eleven plus examination system, which puts them on a sidetrack before they have had the time and the chance to develop and prove their abilities, it does not sound the clarion call for their salvage that one might expect. The report carries a table that shows the percentage of children born in 1940–41 reaching full-time higher education—by father's occupation. Forty-five per cent of the children of the higher professional fathers reached full-time higher education while only two per cent of the children of semi- and unskilled fathers did so. That is, 15,000 upper-class students produced 6,750 university students, but 137,000 lower-class students produced only 2,740 university students. Making every possible allowance for superior nature as well as nurture in the upper-class group, there must be a tremendous wastage of ability in the lower-class group.

Labour-controlled districts such as Greater London, with over eight million population, and Bristol, are moving vigorously to change these ratios by abolishing the eleven plus examinations, withdrawing aid from the 'public' (private) grammar schools, and sending their children to streamed comprehensive schools that have one stream leading to the sixth form. This gives the slower developing child from an impoverished cultural background a chance to make it to the sixth form and later to the university. How fast this movement spreads will determine whether a much larger proportion of the population than the Robbins Report predicts will come knocking at the university doors in the next fifteen years. Unless this great pool of unused ability in the lower classes of the population is piped into the universities they are likely to drop below the critical mass needed for world competition.

Great Britain is about on even terms with other European countries, except the Scandinavian, in the proportion of age groups entering full-time higher education. Robbins cites the 1958–9 figures as Great Britain 7·7, France 9, West Germany 7, Netherlands 6, and Sweden 12. Because the

Robbins Committee considers the American freshman and sophomore college students only equivalent to the sixth form, its figures for the United States include only entrants to the junior year. The United States figure is 30 per cent; that for Russia is 5 per cent. A much larger proportion of British students is in higher education on a part-time basis than in the United States, probably producing a better supply of sub-professionals than in the United States, which is relatively weak in this category.

(III)

The British universities put great stress on the quality of their output, and rightly so. They are intensely anxious to preserve their high standards and are willing to sacrifice other considerations including costs, faculty manpower, and more democratic admissions procedures. Robbins cites an interesting comparison of percentage of B.A.s in Britain with M.A.s in the United States, which would seem to justify the British system. In 1961–62, 5·6 per cent of the age group in Britain completed bachelor's degrees as against 3·4 per cent in the United States completing master's. Robbins considers the British B.A. comparable to the American M.A. degree. However, as the report repeatedly says, such comparisons include differing variables and must be treated with due reserve. One important factor not mentioned is that it is less and less customary in the United States for doctoral candidates to bother with M.A.s except as a consolation.

British universities maintain a lower ratio of students to faculty than any other country. In 1960 the figures are Great Britain 8:1, Sweden 12:1, Russia 12:1, U.S.A. 13:1, Netherlands 14:1, France 30:1, and West Germany 35:1. The British claim not only higher quality of teaching and much less wastage but point out that their university courses are shorter by one to two years than in the other countries. The high student-faculty ratios in France and Germany are a result almost entirely of the lecture system.

English university students are paid to study by a combination of subsidies from their home boards of education and Parliamentary sources. Not only are their fees paid in most cases but subsistence funds for the school year are paid to them, ranging from about $820 a year down to about $600[1] for those from higher income families. These amounts have much greater buying power for student needs than they would have in the United States. In addition there is a grant of thirty pounds for the vacation period. No other country except Russia approaches this kind of student subsidy. Of course this exerts a powerful pull to stay in college with a consequent reduction of wastage. Certainly a great many more students would stay the course in the United States were they fully subsidized.

Lord Fulton, the Sussex Vice-Chancellor, wrote a chapter in the Daiches book entitled 'New Universities in Perspective'. He discusses four questions that the new universities have to answer:

1 Where they should be,
2 How big they should be,
3 What they should teach,
4 How should they teach it.

One of the general conditions laid down was that the new institutions should have campuses of 200 acres or more. This at once dictated a site some distance out in the country. In order to cope with the 'nine-to-five' problem of the Redbrick city universities, residence halls would have to be provided for a considerable proportion of students. Lord Fulton expressed the hope that the U.G.C.'s restriction that no public funds be spent on dormitories would be lifted. The important question of the social cost of universities providing residences is an issue that certainly has different aspects ranging from Oxbridge to London. The new universities have had to expend much of their privately raised capital on student residences.

Many students choose to go away from home to the uni-

[1] Calculated at the pre-devaluation rate of $2.80 to the pound. [Ed.]

versity. The student subsistence allowances make this possible. Therefore the new universities expect to draw nationally distributed student bodies. All of them are located as close as possible to areas that can house their large non-resident student groups. Sussex is particularly fortunate in being so close to Brighton—which is a resort city with much housing empty in the off-season. I think, though, that there must be serious problems of calendar overlap. Probably all the institutions will try to work out ways to let all students reside on campus for at least one year out of three.

The University of Essex has worked out an ingenious scheme for student housing that will require a number of fourteen-story buildings placed in the midst of the academic buildings. The two top floors will houses instructors and married couples. The other twelve will contain thirteen rooms in two groups. Resident students will have study-bedrooms; students living off campus will have rooms for study. There will be kitchenettes in each apartment for breakfast or snacks. In this way students will have a campus home. Classes will run until 7.00 p.m. and restaurants and coffee bars will keep open until a late hour. The campus community will operate day and night. This will be the Essex answer to the 'nine-to-five' problem. The alternate work and study programme, used by several of the colleges of advanced technology, is called in Britain the 'sandwich plan'. The same term seems coming into use to describe the co-education arrangement of alternate floors for men and women.

The planners hope to preserve a healthy balance between the campus and the neighbouring city with many students living there and going there for recreation and cultural activities while townspeople will be welcomed at campus affairs. The academic community will co-operate with the business and industrial community in research, development, and adult education. The hope is for a healthy tension to be created and maintained between the scholarly life and the contemporary world.

Plans for size vary. At Sussex an immediate goal of 3,000 is spoken of and a more distant one of 5,000. At Essex 3,000 is the figure for the first ten years; 6,000 is the figure mentioned for 1980, with 10,000 as a minimum ultimate limit though the architect has been asked to plan so that 20,000 might be reached if necessary. My opinion is that these new universities are going to prove so popular that they will be under the heaviest kind of pressure to expand much more rapidly than they now plan. Of course, if they prove so successful—they are swamped with qualified applicants now—others like them may eventually be built, but during the years until they appear the 'seven brave young Britains' will be under siege.

Socially, though not academically, the new 'U's' already outrank the non-U Redbricks. The educational innovations of the new universities account for part of their pulling power but, to put it frankly, they have snob appeal second only to Oxbridge. Some of the Redbricks, keenly sensitive to the new competition, are moving all or part of their buildings to American-style campuses on the outskirts of their cities. However, the largest of them have heavy financial investments in their smoke- and grime-surrounded city sites. The University of the South West, at Exeter, and Leeds are two examples of new campus development. Exeter, which is still small, had only a few old buildings squeezed into the centre of the city near the cathedral, but has a large area in which to grow, a mile or two from the centre. The push toward the American-style campus is one of the first of the impacts of the new universities on the old system.

Lord Fulton estimates that not less than 350 to 400 teachers would be enough to provide impetus for scholarship and to maintain teaching services. This is his lowest estimate of the critical mass of teachers and researchers necessary for a dynamic university. Since Sussex plans a student-faculty ratio of 8:1 to maintain a tutorial system of instruction, this gives a figure of about 3,000 students as the minimum to be attained as rapidly as possible.

(IV)

What to teach is being answered differently in each of the new universities.[1] Some are going to present a broad spectrum of arts and sciences from the beginning—for example, Sussex. Others, like Essex, preferring large schools with many professors in kindred subjects to stimulate each other, are going for size and depth in only a few schools in the beginning. All will devote some attention initially, and more later, to applied social sciences and technology. Graduate work will be undertaken from the outset. The character of business and industry of each region will influence the subject taught. Essex will have a School of Physical Science because it is close to industry, while East Anglia, its northern neighbour, will balance the curricular equation with a School of Biological Science.

The curricular schemes of the seven represent innovations that will bear close watching by American colleges and universities. All of the new universities will organize their curricula, I believe (though I am not sure about the last ones) into schools of related subjects. This approach lies somewhere between the American method of general education plus specialization in a single subject or discipline and the old British system of deep and narrow concentration in a single subject straight through the three years of the university. It assumes that general education in the broad sense has been accomplished by the end of the sixth form. However, it requires each student to spend a considerable portion of his total study on 'contextual' subjects as well as his special subject.

Specialization in a given type of study, say history, may take place in different schools and within different contexts. Flexibility, rather than the rigidity of the old honours course, will have priority. Students will be permitted to

[1] For a thorough survey, see Malcolm B. Campbell, 'Non-specialist study in the Undergraduate Curricula of the new Universities and Colleges of Advanced Technology in England', University of Michigan Comparative Education Dissertation Series, No. 10, Ann Arbor, Mich., 1966. [Ed.]

change their objectives within a certain range of studies until the end of the first year. Those who do not meet 'university' standards will be transferred to further higher education training in other institutions.

Sussex has begun with the following schools: English and American Studies, European Studies, Social Studies, School of Education and Social Work, School of Asian and African Studies, School of Physical Sciences, and School of Biological Sciences. Essex has begun with only three schools: School of Comparative Studies (Government and Literature), School of Physical Sciences, and School of Social Studies.

The Essex curricular matrix is the simplest and while it is not typical of Sussex or any of the others it is near enough in curricular strategy to be used as an example. Vice-Chancellor Sloman's B.B.C. Reith lectures, upon which I shall draw, explain its principles, selection of schools and subjects, offerings and requirements, and opportunities for both undergraduate and graduate development.

The first principle that he advances, and that is given greater weight at Essex than at Sussex, is the advantage and necessity of big departments. He assumes, as do the other universities, that research is a primary university responsibility. Because modern research requires teams of experts he reasons that departments, especially in science, may have to grow to fifty or more staff members. Big science research projects require large assemblages of expensive and sophisticated equipment that small departments cannot afford. He believes that only when British universities create such powerful departments will government and industry offer them large-scale research contracts such as go to Berkeley or M.I.T. Large departments are magnets for staff because faculty members need and desire the collaboration of eminent scholars. While Sloman grants that big departments are more imperatively needed in science than in the social sciences or the humanities, he cites the latters' growing use of equipment—for example, computers, language laboratories, etc.—and their need for big collections of books and periodicals. The new universities, he believes, can build up large research collections for only a few big departments with strong graduate divisions. The logic of these arguments leads to the grouping of related departments in schools with interlocked curricula and some basic courses taken in common by most or all students. If British universities are to develop departments that can compete nationally and even internationally they must concentrate, à la Montgomery: 'attack on a narrow front, and where there is a breakthrough go hell-bent ahead'.

With big departments the old tradition of one life-time professor at the head must change to a table of organization nearer the American style with many more professors and a rotating chairmanship. Sloman believes that one reason for the 'brain drain' is the frustration of many scientists in being held down in subordinate positions with little hope of advancement.

Students will enter schools rather than departments and take the same series of integrated courses taught collaboratively by the members of the allied departments. Some departments will act as bridges and belong to more than one school. Progress examinations will be held at the end of the first year with an opportunity for a 'resit' in the autumn. Part of the work done during the year will be counted into the examination, which may tend to lessen its terrors.

In the second and third years students will specialize in a given subject though they may surround it with a variety of contextual subjects. (At Sussex each student will prepare for four contextual subjects and five in his special subject. One might study history there, for example, in the School of European History, of English and American History, or of Social Studies, with different specialized content and contextual subjects.)

All students at Essex will be registered for honours courses. No general or pass degree courses will be offered, though an occasional student not found quite up to third-class honours may be awarded a pass degree rather than an outright failure. Senior research projects, major essays and certain other written work will be counted towards the degree examinations.

Essex expects an increasing proportion of B.A.s to go on for another year of graduate work leading to an M.A. or M.Sc. In agreement with one of the Robbins recommendations it will offer course work at the first graduate level. The British university custom has been for graduate students to take no further courses but to engage full time in research. Many master's degree students will be prepared to enter teaching or industrial research or employment at the end of their fourth year. The ablest students interested in a career of scholarship will stay for two more years to work towards a Ph.D. degree and post-doctoral students will be welcomed and provided for. Essex hopes to attract graduate students from other institutions to its big departments.

In deciding on its schools of study, Essex first took into account national need. The U.G.C. made several pointed suggestions, namely that doctors and dentists, veterinarians and agriculturists could be trained in sufficient numbers at existing universities. It advised that Essex begin with the humanities, social sciences, and pure sciences, and later allow the applied sciences to grow from these bases. The needs of the region also were taken into account, including the industries to which the university might be of special aid. A balance of subjects was necessary and desirable between the humanities and the physical sciences, with the social sciences bridging the gap.

The School of Physical Sciences choice 'was determined by regional consideration' because they would provide 'a firm base for the student of electronics and other branches of engineering, which are leading industries in Essex'. A School of Engineering Science is expected to develop from the basic physical sciences of chemistry, mathematics, and physics. The second School of Social Studies very significantly also includes mathematics as well as sociology, economics, government, and later—education. Management studies, which are rare and much needed in England, may develop in this school. The humanities at Essex will at first be confined to the School of Comparative Studies through departments of literature and government. The overlap of government in the latter two schools is to be noted. Contemporary and international approaches will focus on Russia, North America and Latin America, and perhaps later the Far East. It is hoped that the unusual combination of literature and government will prove mutually stimulating.

Two special features of Essex will be a Language Centre and a Creative Arts Centre. All students will be encouraged and many required to study at least one language. Six or seven languages will be taught, including English for foreigners, plus applied linguistics and new methods of teaching languages. Plans for the art centre are still in the making, on the principle that the university should provide a place for the creative artist as well as the critic.

The new universities, from York and Lancaster in the north to Sussex and Kent in the south, were made free by the U.G.C. within very wide limits to select and arrange their own departments and schools of studies. The Essex scheme in originality and adaptation to its region is a good example, I think, of the new approach to curricular structure in England today. The Sussex scheme is more suggestive of the American liberal arts college but perhaps some of our colleges might do better work by specializing in fewer subjects. The methods of teaching in the new universities will differ considerably and will range from the almost pure tutorial system of Sussex to the Essex plan of very large lecture groups supported by many small classes or seminars of about ten students each. The intention at Essex is to have no small lecture classes. In all the new foundations, and in the recommendations of the Robbins Report for the future, there is a firm intention to keep the student-faculty ratio low, at about the figure 8:1, which presently holds. This generous provision of teachers using tutorial methods to a large extent has made the British universities the best in the world up to the B.A. degree. Because they have given much less attention and support to graduate work it is generally recognized that American universities have surpassed them in this respect. No less an authority than C. P. Snow supports this view.

The question for the future is whether Britain can afford to maintain as low a student-faculty ratio as 8:1. The nearest other countries come to it is the 12:1 for Sweden and Russia and the 13:1 for the United States. Taking into account Britain's comparatively slender personnel resources and the incoming larger numbers of university students, which the Robbins Report may have underestimated, there are certainly grounds for grave doubts that the 8:1 ratio can be maintained.

When I raised this question with Lord Fulton he staunchly defended the tutorial system but he granted that some retreat from it might eventually be necessary. In making this reluctant concession, though, he made a very significant statement that I had heartily to agree with. 'If and when we have to retreat from the tutorial system as now planned, we shall do it from the top down, because the new students have the greatest need for it and that is where the investment is most fruitful. The older and more experienced the student the more capable of independent study he should be.' This strong statement coming from one of the foremost university innovators and administrators in England should attract prayerful attention in the United States where even in some of our 'small' colleges we are herding freshmen into large classes.

The governmental structure of the new universities, which are all ultimately dependent on the approval and the financing of U.G.C., does not differ markedly from the Redbrick model, which is based on a large Court of several hundred eminent people, mostly from the immediate region, with important representation of faculty, a smaller council, a faculty senate, and school and department boards. (The ancient universities of Oxford and Cambridge are governed solely by their own academic bodies.) Usually the Court is the supreme authority, though Essex is making the Council supreme in all except the appointment of the

Chancellor, the Vice-Chancellor, and public members of the Council. At Essex there will be student representatives on the Court. The big difference in university government between the British and American systems is, of course, the presence on the supreme body of a large faculty delegation in Britain and its complete absence in most American universities. Another great difference, of course, is the buffer state that the U.G.C. interposes between Parliament (and politics) and the universities. The British universities have been free to a remarkable extent from interference with their academic freedom by industry, business, or politics.

(V)

Because the new universities were planned from scratch, the planners and architects had an unusual and challenging opportunity to relate their programmes and personnel to sites in rational and aesthetic patterns. While probably they cannot solve the parking problem that has beset American universities, at least they have been able to attack it on a broad front. At Essex the architects have ingeniously built the major building over a ravine through which the wheeled traffic will be completely separated from the pedestrians. At Sussex, Essex, and York the living and social quarters and academic buildings have been cleverly arranged in close contact with each other with the aim of creating busy and vital communities, active through most of the hours of the night as well as the nine-to-five day. Vice-Chancellor Sloman at Essex plans for a closely knit community on a relatively small section of the total university property rather than for 'pavilions in a park'. With three lakes down the centre, the third of which is just being built, the total campus prospect should be both beautiful and dramatic. The academic buildings will be of white concrete and the first tall residence towers an exciting blue brick. (Incidentally, the new universities are being referred to in some quarters as the Whitebricks to differentiate them from the Redbricks; but they will wear variegated architectural robes.)

47

The open end of the campus points towards the city of Colchester, which will soon grow out to meet it. The university of Sussex is planned in a series of connected courts into which no cars can penetrate and gives promise of presenting a muscular and interesting, though less concentrated, mass than Essex.

The Oxford and Cambridge college system in which all students reside and eat their meals in their own building has been departed from in all the new universities I have seen or read about. It is too expensive a method to continue. In no case do the planners expect to provide housing for all students. The Essex plan with its study rooms for off-campus residents comes closest to full residence.

The planning by the U.G.C. of the seven new universities preceded the Robbins Committee Report, but both groups planned on a national and long-range scale that our much greater size and Constitutional limitations have kept us from doing. The Robbins visitors to the United States were much impressed by the comprehensive plan and organization of California's higher educational system and expressed the opinion that other states may have to emulate it.

The bold and original planning of the 'seven brave new Britains' is already having a powerful impact on the British university system. No doubt it will be observed and emulated to some extent in other Commonwealth countries and perhaps in the United States. While probably we cannot import any of its innovations without extensive adaptation to our different needs and conditions, we certainly should examine them with intense interest and respect.

SOME PROBLEMS OF NEW UNIVERSITIES IN ENGLAND

Wilfrid Harrison
Pro Vice-Chancellor
The University of Warwick

Today there are many new universities scattered widely over the world—Bochum in Germany, for example, Macquarie in Australia, Trent in Canada, Jodhpur in India. This paper does not deal with the problems of all new universities. It is confined to the problems of a particular group of universities in England which, in recent years, have come to be known collectively as 'the new universities'. This group is composed of the universities of Sussex (1961), East Anglia (1963), York (1963), Lancaster (1964), Essex (1964), Kent at Canterbury (1965) and Warwick (1965).[1] (The dates are those of the first admissions of students.)

Why these universities may be regarded as constituting a group will become apparent in what follows. Why I write about their problems will be obvious already: I work in one of them. This by no means makes me an authority even on my own university, and I am certainly not an authority on the other six, only four of which, indeed, I have contrived to visit. I have, however, had the benefit of conversations with members of all the universities in the group; and while I am very conscious that my account refers mainly to problems of which I have become aware as the result of personal experience, I think that all of these problems have been encountered in one form or another by the other universities.

[1] The University of Keele is not included in this group, although its Charter was granted in 1962, because it began, as the University College of North Staffordshire, in 1950. On the importance of its example, see page 68, n.1.

(I)

The uniqueness of these new universities should not be exaggerated. Apart from Oxford and Cambridge and the four ancient Scottish universities, all British universities are in some sense new. Most of the English civic universities obtained charters in the present century. New university colleges were created in almost every decade between the 1820s (St. David's College, Lampeter, 1822), and the 1950s (Sussex, 1959). Starting new places of higher learning might indeed be said to be a well-established British tradition; and it could be added that, as a consequence, what is started in such places cannot now be entirely novel, whether in physical shape or in curricula. Some innovations can be made, but there can scarcely be scope for revolutions.

The new universities with which I am concerned nonetheless exhibit certain unusual features. They were all made universities before they began their operations, and did not first serve apprenticeships as university colleges (Sussex obtained a Charter before its first students were admitted). They have tended to become thought of, and to some extent have also tended to think of themselves, as a very distinct group, partly, no doubt, because they all began as universities, but partly also because their starting dates fell within one short five-year period. In the middle of this period, moreover, the Robbins Committee[1] reported (1963) and the new universities have tended to be thought of, even more than the new technological universities (the former colleges of advanced technology) have been thought of, as 'Robbins Universities'. Again, they have probably also

[1] The terms of reference of the Committee were—'to review the pattern of full-time higher education in Great Britain and in the light of national needs and resources to advise Her Majesty's Government on what principles its long-term development should be based. In particular, to advise, in the light of these principles, whether there should be any changes in that pattern, whether any new types of institution are desirable and whether any modification should be made in the present arrangements for planning and co-ordinating the development of the various types of institution'.

tended to think of themselves in this way, as beneficiaries of the Robbins Committee's proposals for expansion, and as pioneers in carrying out certain principles endorsed by the Committee, notably those of broadening first degree courses, having higher proportions of graduate students, and having more extensive participation by non-professorial academic staff in university government. Finally the apparent suddenness of their creation, their apparent relation to Robbins, and, to some extent, their own concern with publicity, have made them, in a period of great general activity in education and greatly expanded public expenditure on education, objects of perhaps more than their fair share of attention in the national Press.

The fundamental problem of this kind of new university is that it wants to develop quickly in a highly competitive educational world in which the public authorities are by no means committed to favouring newer as against older institutions of learning, or, for that matter, to favouring universities as against other institutions of higher education. The new university wants to develop quickly for at least three reasons. First, it has attracted enthusiastic and generally fairly young academic staff, anxious to show how they can develop their subjects and convinced of the need for first-class equipment and facilities. Secondly, it is often thought, rightly or wrongly, that advance should be as rapid as possible as an insurance against the possibility of later standstill. Thirdly, it is frequently thought that if a university advances rapidly it may in so doing demonstrate its suitability as a candidate for support from both public and private funds for yet further advance.

(II)

With this broad general problem constantly in mind, the new university must from the beginning face a series of more particular problems, all of which are affected, in its first few years, by the fact that it must come into operation in stages. To begin with, a local Promotion Committee makes a case for having a university on a particular site. If this achieves government approval, then it can be assumed that in due course a Charter will be granted. The first thoughts about the nature of the university and what it will do are given by an Academic Planning Board containing representatives of established universities. Then at a point of time at which, strictly speaking, there is still no university at all, a vice-chancellor and registrar are appointed. These will be joined by other administrative officials, and then, perhaps two years before the first undergraduate students are due to arrive, the appointments of the first persons to professorships will be made, although the persons then appointed may not proceed to take up office for several months. Before this, obviously, some decisions will already have been taken in conjunction with the advisory Academic Planning Board. It will have been decided what the first subjects to be professed in the university will be, and this will have involved the first steps in planning the use of the site. The outlines of a university constitution will have begun to be considered. The lines for an appeal for financial support will have been under discussion.

More than one consideration must underlie the choice of subjects, and it affects fairly equally schemes for undergraduate courses and schemes for research. No new university is likely to wish to appear to be unbalanced, to have, for example, huge science departments and negligible arts departments, or to have the opposite. At the same time it would be undesirable to try to offer too wide a range of subjects, and it would be foolish to offer too narrow a range. Certain subjects can scarcely be omitted: it seems extremely unlikely that any modern British university would decide to dispense with either English or mathematics. On the other hand the demand for certain other subjects—the classics, for instance—may be thought to be quite sufficiently well catered for in existing universities. Some subjects, again, particularly nuclear physics, are likely to be out of the question because they are too expensive. Others may be hard to contemplate in advance of fairly long discussions and negotiations with outside bodies: medicine and architecture are in this position. The geographical location of the site may be favourable or unfavourable to a particular subject: engineering science is probably most likely to develop successfully in a university in, or adjacent to, an industrial area. Trends of public opinion and of government policy must also be taken into account: what a university does must in some measure respond to accepted conceptions of national requirements. What the university proposes to do in the light of these various considerations must then be phased, but it must begin with a reasonable spread of subjects reasonably manned.

Views on points such as these will have determined the choice of the first professors, not only with reference to the subjects they will profess, but also with reference to their particular interests in those subjects. There is then still very much more to be done, and to be done under somewhat awkward conditions. It is unlikely that all of the first professors will already know one another; it is not impossible, indeed, that no one of them will know any of the others. They will come from different backgrounds and with different kinds of academic experience, some, say, from Oxford or Cambridge, some from civic universities, some from Commonwealth or foreign universities, some, perhaps, with considerable experience of university administration, some with little or none. They have to explain their aims to one another, they have to explore what is involved in co-operation between subjects and determining how scarce resources are to be allocated. They find themselves invited to comment upon a draft constitution. They may even have to learn how to follow constitutional procedures. Much of this must begin before the professors can take up office, while they have continuing duties in other places and can meet together only from time to time. It is not surprising, therefore, that when the first undergraduates are due to arrive much that is required for the first year may still not have been finished. Most of the non-professorial academic staff (again, in general, strangers to one another) will probably not have arrived very long before the undergraduates. The full apparatus of senate and other bodies cannot come into operation until this stage.

The first year of the new university will add its own special difficulties. The necessary buildings may not be ready in time. The student body consists of first year undergraduates and some graduates. There are no second and third year undergraduates to guide the freshmen, and the new students have to try to work out for themselves what their roles should be. Simultaneously the various boards and committees which administer the university are beginning to operate with no traditions behind them, and, in many cases, with some very inexperienced members serving on them. New first year undergraduate courses are being given. Applicants for posts in the second academic year are being interviewed, and in some cases it may not be possible to settle the full details of second year courses until appointments for that year have been made and the persons appointed have been consulted. Buildings for occupation in that year are in the course of erection and the building requirements of subsequent years are being planned. In the second academic year, perhaps, the numbers of students and of academic staff are to double, and in the following year as many again are to be added. In both years, perhaps, new subjects are to be introduced, and it is hoped to rectify some of the mistakes that will inevitably have been made in the first year. So the work of the first year is undertaken in the knowledge that for two more years at the very least the problems of assimilation, and no doubt also those of improvization, may be expected to continue.

(III)

In addition to the internal problems that have so far been outlined, there are external problems, some of which give rise to yet further internal problems. A university must attract students. It must seek to establish and maintain good relations with neighbouring local authorities and with the community round about. It must consider its relations with other universities and it must deal with central bodies, and, in particular, with the University Grants Committee.

In general it is not difficult for a new university to attract undergraduates. Many schoolboys and schoolgirls appear to be attracted by the new universities, for a variety of reasons, some sound and some not. They may think that entrance standards will not be very rigorous. They may think that in the earlier years students will be accorded more individual attention than they would be accorded in larger institutions. They may expect that the staff will be younger on average than in other places, less orthodox, more experimental, more permissive. They may expect the courses to be 'exciting'. Some of them may look forward to becoming leaders in the student body more quickly than they could expect to do in a larger and longer-established university. They may expect that their fellow students, just because they too have been attracted to a new university, will, like themselves, be livelier and more interesting than most students. For at least these reasons the new university will not be short of applicants. But one qualification should be made. In the case of the physical sciences applications may be disappointing in the first year, for one very obvious cause: schoolmasters and schoolmistresses may have warned their sixth-formers that a new university cannot be expected to have laboratory facilities as good as those in more developed universities.

Some disadvantages may also arise because of some of the applicants' expectations. Prospectuses and other forms of publicity convey brand images. One can scarcely say in the first prospectus: 'We hope that the first building will be ready in time, and that transport and facilities for sports will be adequate'. It is necessary to be more positive, and even when it is not intended, some degree of exaggeration may creep in: courses of study may be indicated before they have been planned in much detail, or there may have been assumptions that were too optimistic about the availability of special staff or special facilities that the courses will

E

require: architects' drawings in a prospectus may convey the impression that buildings will be more commodious than they turn out to be when they are finished. The atmosphere of the university which the students find may seem to them not to warrant the enthusiasm that was evident in the accounts they earlier read. Partly for these reasons, and partly for other more familiar reasons (such as that it is very difficult for any sixth former to foresee in advance what he will encounter in a university—including the other ex-sixth-formers) the very success of the new university in attracting undergraduates may itself create some difficulties of disillusionment.

How successful a new university will be in attracting graduate students will depend upon a number of different factors. At the very beginning it may be able to attract very few indeed, apart from some locally recruited part-time graduate students, except those who have already begun to work with its professors and lecturers in their former universities and now elect to move with them. If the last group is large in any subject then the nucleus of a graduate school in that subject may be quickly formed. Otherwise a subject must depend on success in approaches for outside financial support for its research projects, and for some subjects, particularly in the natural sciences, success may come quite early. But there is still the question of securing awards for applicants, and it is unlikely that a new university will have many of its own to offer. The applicant must then look to one of the research councils, or, for research in arts subjects, to the Department of Education and Science. Science and social studies applicants will know that in general the older universities will receive most of the earmarked awards of the research councils and most of them will therefore prefer to apply to be named for awards by those universities. The arts students, to whom the awards of the Department of Education and Science are made personally, may elect to hold their awards at a new university if they are attracted by its accounts of its courses and the reputation of its staff. But they will know that its library cannot contain much research material, and arts students obtain proportionately fewer awards than do science students.

The difficulties of the graduate students who come to a new university are probably fewer than those of the undergraduate students. The graduate student has a better idea of what he is doing and why he has made his choice of university. In the very first year of a new university, however, they may experience certain difficulties. They may feel socially isolated when there are no other students between them and an undergraduate first year. They are also likely to be more conscious than the undergraduates will be of deficiencies in facilities: they will be more conscious of the shortage of academic accommodation, and they may well find the library disappointing.

A local authority or local authorities will have been represented on the Promotion Committee which sought approval for the establishment of the new university. It, or they, will have been concerned in obtaining the site. The development plan for the site must be approved by a local Council in its capacity as a planning authority: so must the separate building projects, as these come forward. The permanency of the links between neighbouring local authorities and universities is also likely to be symbolized by the fact that the local authorities will nominate certain of the members who sit on the Council and the Court of the university.

It is not possible to venture on generalizations about the actual relations between new universities and local authorities, but it is clear that a local authority can be of great help to a university and that equally it can be of considerable hindrance. Planning permission might proceed smoothly or it might not. A local authority might help readily or it might not help very readily over many other matters, for instance, over access roads, the provision of lighting or paving on existing approach roads, the provision of 'bus services, 'bus stops, 'bus shelters, traffic lights, crossings, water supply, sewage disposal.

These, of course, are features that obtain for most older universities. But they obtain in a special way for the new university. As with undergraduate students, so it could be with local authorities: difficulties could arise in their relations with a new university, because expectation and realization did not match. It is likely that the local authorities in whose territories the new universities are located have not had previous experience of universities sited within their areas. They have dealt with schools, and area or regional colleges, possibly colleges of education, and housing estates. On the other side most of the staff of new universities are likely to have come from older universities where relations with local authorities have been so long established that to a large extent they have ceased to be noticed, at least by many academics. In these circumstances misunderstandings could arise on both sides. Local councillors and officials could entertain false hopes about the kinds of benefits a university could bring to their area. Members of the university might be surprised to find that the university had to seek permission from the local authority for some of the things it wanted to do. They might be surprised, too, to find that there was a tendency on the part of councillors and officials to look on the university as a new local or regional institution rather than as the national or even international institution the members of the university considered it to be.

There are obviously many matters on which misunderstandings might arise. Such misunderstandings, however, are by no means inevitable, and in general one is aware of mutual benefits rather than of mutual misunderstandings. Many examples could certainly be cited of the very considerable generosity extended to the new universities by their neighbouring local authorities, and the benefits the universities derive in this way are direct and evident. On the other hand the benefits that the universities can bestow are less direct and obvious because they affect the local communities rather than the local authorities as such. Perhaps, therefore, if there are possibilities of misunderstandings, the onus for avoiding them lies with the members of the university. They should be alert and look in advance for possible points of sensitivity. They should be tactful (if they can be: universities are not always the best of training schools in tact). They should also try to encourage their students to be tactful, outside the university precincts as well as inside.

Neighbouring schools and colleges are unlikely to present problems. Indeed the coming of a university provides an answer to some of the problems of schools and colleges. Vice-Chancellors and professors are gifts from Providence to headmasters and headmistresses who have exhausted the list of other notables for speech days. They and their colleagues will be very welcome on such occasions as sixth-form conferences. They provide a new source of supply of governors. They may be induced to hold conferences with headmasters and headmistresses on questions of joint interest to schools and universities. They may arrange public lectures in the university which the pupils of neighbouring schools can attend. They may organize refresher courses for teachers. They may enrol teachers and lecturers in neighbouring schools and colleges as part-time research students. They may be able to help the colleges with occasional lectures and seminars, or, if it can be managed, by allowing access to the library.

These are immediate, and important, ways in which the new university can be seen to bring benefits to the surrounding community. With variations, similar kinds of benefits can arise from the contacts between a new university and many kinds of voluntary organizations. They will arise, too, with industry, if parts of the work of the university are of a kind in which industry is interested. In these various ways considerable goodwill towards the new university can be developed locally.

The university must also have regard, however, to another important section of the neighbouring community—the individual householders who may be willing to accept students as lodgers. The dimensions of lodgings problems must vary considerably as between the different new universities. Some—for instance Sussex, Lancaster and Essex

—are within travelling distance of coast resorts where accommodation may be available for students outside holiday seasons. Others are in areas where there is little tradition of letting lodgings, and when, perhaps, earnings are such that there is little incentive to add to them by 'taking people in'. For such universities, at least, a great deal of effort must be put into ensuring adequate accommodation for students, especially when the capital grants available and the sums that can be spent from an appeal fund can provide accommodation in halls of residence for only a minority of the students. Possible landlords and landladies must be sought out and must be encouraged by all the means an active lodgings officer can devise—by advertisements and press announcements, by personal visits, by talks to as many of the relevant voluntary organizations as possible. When lodgings have been found and students have been allocated to them every effort must be made to ensure that good relations between the students and the householders are maintained. In many cases students are excellent ambassadors for the university: in some cases they are far from being so, and it may be necessary on occasion to remind a student that the university would find it much easier to replace him than it would to replace his landlady.

Relations with the local Press must be considered. It is from the local newspapers that the majority of the inhabitants in the area will gain their impressions of the university, and at least during its early years a new university is likely to be given more attention in local newspapers than would a more established university that had come to be taken for granted. Many routine matters will cause no difficulties. Photographs of progress with buildings, announcements of new developments and new appointments or of research grants received are all acceptable and helpful. But the Press can also spread less welcome news, particularly in connection with the behaviour of students, and this is again a matter on which some students, especially inexperienced students, may have to be advised or warned. The public image of a university should not be based upon the impressions made by its more thoughtless junior members, but it may well be so based if steps are not taken to render such junior members more thoughtful, and especially those of them who hold office in student organizations.

In the very early stages of the new university there is yet another reason why the students should make a good impression in the surrounding community: they can be helped by being lent sports facilities at a time when these cannot be provided by the university. It is not likely that a new university can afford to devote much of its capital allocation or much from its appeal fund to the provision of pitches, changing rooms, tennis courts or squash courts. In some cases, moreover, even if the funds were available, the amount of work that has to be done (for instance, in the levelling and draining of land intended for pitches) could mean that it will take many months before facilities are ready. The loan of facilities by neighbouring clubs can thus be very welcome indeed and it is of great importance that the best of relations with such bodies should be maintained.

(IV)

These questions of the relations between the new university and its local neighbours turn to quite an extent on the image of the new university that becomes established. To some extent the relations between the new university and other universities will also turn on questions of images. The older universities cannot be said to have given a unanimous welcome to the new universities. It has not seemed self-evident to them that only by creating new universities could rising numbers of students be dealt with. Nor has it seemed self-evident to them that it is more economical to create completely new sets of buildings, libraries and laboratories than to extend existing buildings, libraries and laboratories. It has been no more clear that older universities should be expected to welcome the creation of new graduate schools when many of the older universities have themselves still been engaged in building up their own graduate schools. Why, in particular, should they be enthusiastic if the first research students attracted to the new graduate schools include their own best graduates ? Again, the new universities have, at least in theory, been allowed some latitude in their earlier years in their ratios of staff to students and of senior to junior staff. They have certainly drawn away promising members of staff, both academic and administrative, from the older universities in times when replacements have not been easy to find, and some of the members of staff concerned have obtained a rapidity of promotion in these transfers that might otherwise not have been possible for them. (This is epitomized in a formula used by some members of older universities in extreme cases—'He would never have got a Chair *here*!') The new universities have also added to the competition for the best undergraduate students, and some of them, in doing so, have appeared to be ready to lower entrance requirements.

But further, in their zeal for rapid expansion some of the new universities, perhaps all of them, have appeared to some people in the older universities to be ready to abandon dignity, or solidity, or both, in order to maximize their attractions. What to enthusiasts inside the new universities has been no more than a healthy concern to experiment and to innovate could then seem to many in the older universities to be a preoccupation with 'gimmicks'. Everything in the new university, it has appeared to some critics, must be different. Buildings must be unlike those of existing universities. The constitutions of the new universities must be different: they would have, perhaps, no faculties, or no deans, or no departments, they will have 'colleges' even before they have buildings, or they will have a unitary organization but no students' union. There will also be a great deal of emphasis on the importance of direct democracy in university government. The syllabuses would be different: perhaps old subjects would have new names, or new subjects would be compounded out of parts of old subjects, or familiar subjects would be taken in unfamiliar combinations, and some well-established old subjects would not be there at all. The prospectuses would be glossy and illustrated, even if the photographs in the first issues had to be those of local ancient monuments or of some empty fields described as 'part of the university site'. There would be new and 'exciting' teaching methods and the relations between staff and students would be new and exciting. To match all this the academic staff would include people who had been thought of as not quite sound in the places they came from, although admittedly they could be counted on to be active in public relations; and one could expect there to be students in parallel, anxious to be in the new universities vogue, and to be trend-leaders in some new society they would suppose that the new universities would help to create.

Perhaps no one person in any of the older universities has actually entertained all of these views; but all of them have been entertained by some people in the older universities. Many of these views involve some unfairness. The new universities, for instance, could not have started at all if they had not been able to attract staff from existing universities. And the constitutional and other innovations indicated are not all of them peculiar to the new universities. Modifications had begun to be made in the older universities in both their structures of government and their degree structures before the new universities came into being. Many of the older universities became less authoritarian, they made provision for greater participation in university affairs on the part of junior academic staff, they began to break down barriers between departments and to introduce 'interdisciplinary' degrees and new teaching methods. In these directions they naturally moved more slowly than new universities have been able to move, partly because there was some internal resistance to such changes, but partly also because it is always more difficult to change complicated existing arrangements than it is to create new arrangements where none have existed before. Even so, many of the older universities have in recent years issued publications much glossier than those with which they were formerly content.[1] It should be added, moreover, that the extent to which the new universities may really have 'tried to be different' was in some measure forced upon them. Why should anyone choose to go to a new university if it had nothing distinctive to offer? And how can a new university develop research if it remains entirely in fields that are already well-cultivated in other places?

But while there can thus be a degree of unfairness in some of the criticisms levelled at the new universities from inside the older universities, some of the resentment in the new universities at such criticism is itself not entirely well-founded. Many of the academic staff in the new institutions have come to them, perhaps, because the speed of change in their former institutions was not fast enough for them. They should not forget, however, that most of the changes they have wished to speed are not of their own invention: they have been based upon changes already beginning elsewhere. If on occasion their statements may seem to imply that they have forgotten this, then it is not surprising that they are sometimes regarded with scepticism. They should notice,

[1] One should mention as an important element in the background influences at work in common on both older and newer universities, the example of an earlier 'new university'—Keele—established as the University College of North Staffordshire in 1949 and granted a Charter in 1962. The establishment of Keele and many of the ideas put into operation there bore the imprint of its first head, Lord Lindsay, formerly Master of Balliol College, Oxford. Lindsay's influence may have extended also to Sussex through its first Vice-Chancellor, John Fulton (now Lord Fulton), who was a colleague of Lindsay's in Balliol. Most of the general influence of Keele has probably arisen from the conceptions embodied in its device of a first (or 'Foundation') year which involves a common core course for all students and postpones the choice of specialization until a student has become familiar with some subjects he had not followed, or indeed, could not have been offered, in his later years at school. But other universities have not copied the Keele device of a four-year first degree course (of which the Foundation Year is the first year); nor have they sought, as Keele sought, to be completely residential for both staff and students.

too, that the sensible desire not to overlap with or duplicate other places in fields of research can lead, if one is not careful, to a form of specialization that can appear to outsiders as eccentric.

However, one would be guilty of exaggeration if the impression we left that all, or even most, of the staff of the new universities have been self-conscious reformers of the kind indicated. Not all of those who have come to new universities have done so in order to lead crusades for innovation. Some have just sought and gained promotion. Some have had a preference for working in a smaller academic community. Some, perhaps, have had a liking for the area in which a particular new university was situated. And some may even have thought that in the peculiar circumstances of a new university there was an interesting opportunity for the exercise of administrative skill.

In the relations between the new universities themselves there has been some comparing of notes, not very highly organized—there is too much to be done in each to make frequent or extended consultation possible. There has no doubt also been some mutual watchfulness and perhaps even, at times, some mutual jealousy. There has been a degree of unnecessary anxiety lest any one of them should be thought by the outside world to be accepted as setting the pattern for the others; and, if so, this too could have helped to give rise to the concern to exhibit distinctiveness which could be interpreted from outside as the desire just to be different. But to say this is to say no more than that between the new universities there is a degree of competition and rivalry that is similar to that which obtains between the other groups of universities. This is to be preferred to the establishment of any sort of union or league of the new universities against the rest.

(V)

In relation to the University Grants Committee, however, the new universities do have certain problems in common although they do not take action in common about these problems. The problems in question arise in a time of financial stringency when the University Grants Committee must act as an agent for government economy.

A new university wishes to develop quickly, in order to become, in the fashionable phrase, 'viable'. (What viability involves by way of student population may be a matter for dispute: some would say a total of 5,000 students, some would say over 5,000, some would say not more than, perhaps, 3,000.)[1] But if a university is to develop quickly, two things must be clear: there must be certainty that the necessary numbers of students will be coming forward, and it also must be possible to count on the necessary capital and recurrent grants. On neither of these questions is there certainty.

A forecast of the growth of the demand for student places was made by the Robbins Committee. This forecast was made the basis of government policy for university expansion. Since the report of the Committee further statistical enquiries have been made, and it has become clear that in the light of newer data the Robbins figures are underestimates. Those figures have nonetheless continued to be used as the basis of government policy. As a consequence the actual expansion to be expected over the period 1967–72 would, if evenly spread over all the universities in the country, require very small additions of intake by each separate university. It is most unlikely that an even spread of this kind will be required. Some universities may remain stationary, some may expand very little, and some may even have to contract, and it may be expected that at least the newer of the new universities will be allowed to have considerably more than an arithmetical 'fair share' of the expansion because such a share would mean that their development would be arrested sadly beneath even the lowest figure estimated for viability. On the other hand these

[1] Ideas of scale change. Birmingham, regarded as a large university, had only 4,947 full-time students in 1963. Ten years ago the figure was about 3,000. Birmingham's Charter was granted in 1900.

universities cannot foresee their growth very clearly. In addition to not knowing how the intake to universities will be shared between the older universities, the new technological universities and themselves, they do not know to what extent in the future school-leavers who wish to proceed to degrees may be encouraged to do so through the colleges of education (to B.Ed. degrees) or through the new 'polytechnics' and other technical colleges which will prepare increasing numbers for the degrees awarded by the Council for National Academic Awards.

These uncertainties the new universities naturally share with the older universities; but whereas the older universities already have capacity for dealing with large numbers, the new universities have not yet achieved such capacity. Again, on the relatively short-term scale on which capital allocations are made, in which no university can know for very far ahead what its capacity will be, in the case of the new university the position has special complications. The new university, for instance, knows much less exactly what the limits of the lodgings accommodation in its area may be expected to be. Full surveys of such accommodation are not reliable if made too far in advance of actual calls on lodgings. Again, the peculiarities of the locations of the sites of the new universities may mean that many more lodgings could be made available if new public transport routes could be brought into operation, but how feasible it may be to get new routes established is not easy to determine. (It is obviously more feasible if students can travel at off-peak periods; but if there is a shortage of teaching space then the difficulties of timetabling may make it impossible to avoid requiring students to travel at peak periods.) The new university is therefore likely to have to insure against a shortage of lodgings by devoting an adequate proportion of its capital allocation to the provision of its own residential accommodation; and again, since it is necessary to keep the students so far as possible on the site throughout the day, because of the pressure of work, and because in so many cases lodgings may supply only breakfast, it is necessary to devote a further part of the capital allocation to the provision of restaurants and working space for students. As a result, the funds available for academic building are reduced.

In these circumstances the planning of developments becomes hazardous. The less the accommodation that is available for academic purposes the smaller the student population must be. But, broadly speaking, the funds are given in relation to student population. Therefore it becomes necessary to strike a balance. Overcrowding must be avoided, but unused capacity or under-use of capacity must also be avoided, and so must a shortfall on intake. But if intake targets are maintained with discomfort in accommodation that is more restricted than a university at first claimed was the minimum it required, then that university runs the risk of being accused of having overestimated and perhaps of being prone to overestimate. To strike the right balance is, then, difficult. The tendency is likely to be to aim at erring a little but not too much on the side of overcrowding academic buildings; and with such a policy there are obvious risks, not the least those arising from the dangers of building delays, the consequences of which could be very much more serious in a new than in a developed university. In the developed university, if a new building is not ready in time it is likely that a prolongation of overcrowding has to be tolerated but work can continue; in a new university such delay could mean that some new subject could not be started at all.

But the difficulties in this field have not yet been set out fully. The development of the site of a new university involves much more than the erection of buildings. Roads have to be laid down and services have to be brought to the new buildings, sometimes over considerable distances. A much greater proportion of the costs of building operations must go into this kind of work on new sites than would have to go into it on developed sites. This is another requirement, then, that makes large inroads into building allocations; and it carries yet another difficulty. Each new site has its own peculiar features. One site may present problems of access for vehicles. Another may involve awkward contours. On others the main difficulties may be flood areas or sewage disposal. Some universities may have to make very large contributions to bring main services to the site. Others may, by a more fortunate geographical position, be able to connect cheaply to existing supplies. If the approvals given to proposed site works take such special features into account then all may be well. But if they are given on the basis of some conception of standard average costs, then some universities may suffer very seriously.

Again, the new university may very well suffer in its building programme just because of its concern to move quickly. More is entailed in this than the risk, already referred to, that buildings may not be ready on time. When there is haste, consultations with those who are to use a building, with the University Grants Committee, and with architects, could be conducted too hurriedly, especially when the attempt is made to deal with many projects simultaneously and the staff that deals with these projects is not very numerous. It may become necessary at a later stage to choose between accepting a finished building with unsatisfactory features and facing extra costs that would arise from, for instance, variations of contracts. Extra costs may also arise, of course, from pressure on contractors to finish on time.

Such questions arise constantly in the short run. At the same time decisions have to be taken about the longer run, and whatever assumptions are made about the longer run may be wrong. Suppose that capital grants are made on the general understanding that a new university may expect to achieve a student population of 3,000 by the end of its first six years. Suppose, too, that in the university itself it is held that there should be considerable further growth after the first six years, but there is no certainty that this view will be accepted. Various kinds of difficulties can then arise. If the buildings required to deal with 3,000 students are designed to do so exactly, then by the time they are ready there will be no room for any additional increase of student numbers. If it seems clear that at least certain subjects are very likely to be able to continue to expand after the sixth year and it is therefore decided to design the buildings for these subjects so as to allow for such expansion, then this can be done only at the cost of holding back some other subjects. If it is decided to restrict the site development generally to what is necessary to meet the demands of a student population of 3,000, the buildings will be grouped close together and the provision of drains, heating, mains and other services will be made to match. But if it later turns out that development beyond 3,000 is to be possible, then the building extension that will be needed must now take place in the periphery and be very expensive; and the services will also have to be expanded: six-inch drains, for instance, may have to be dug up and replaced by ten-inch drains. The preferable alternative would be to place the initial buildings farther apart in order to allow space for later extensions and to plan the various services from the beginning on a scale adequate for such extensions. But this encounters two major obstacles. It could be done only with higher grants if plans for the first 3,000 students were to be adhered to, and it is scarcely likely to be possible if acceptance in principle of the proposal to grow beyond 3,000 students has not been forthcoming.

These difficulties on the capital side have counterparts on the side of recurrent grants. The estimating of recurrent costs is difficult in a new university. On the occasion of the very first estimates there are no previous years to compare and there are sharp limits to the relevance of experience of other universities; and in the first stages of the new university's life each year is still unique. The attempt at an early stage to frame quinquennial estimates is particularly difficult. On the other hand the new university which begins in the course of a quinquennium and has to operate for a year or two on annual grants cannot see its way very clearly. Estimates in the early years of the maintenance costs of the new buildings and of the cost of heating and lighting such buildings are not likely to be very reliable. Yet, budgets must be prepared for these items and they must be considered along with the claims of academics, all of whom have their ambitions for their subjects, and many of whom may consider that in their previous universities there were parsimonious practices that must at all costs be avoided in their new university.

The claims on recurrent grants in the new university also involve a further special feature in the earlier years. In any new institution that is both providing itself with a physical home and establishing its procedures the proportion of administrators to other staff must be higher than it will be ten or twenty years later, and the costs of administration must also be proportionately higher. What is spent on administration cannot be spent on other activities that most academics quite rightly regard as constituting the primary business of the university. On the other hand, the primary business of the university cannot be undertaken at all if procedures are not attended to, and it would be undertaken inefficiently if a shortage of administrative staff meant that procedures were inadequately devised and maintained. Few academics would be so extreme as to question these general propositions, but, like their counterparts in other organizations, they encounter, of course, not general propositions but actual administrators and actual costs of administration; and, again, as in other organizations, it is not a simple matter to attempt to demonstrate to the non-administrator that any particular size of administrative team or level of administrative costs is a necessary minimum. So for reasons somewhat similar to those which may lead to erring on the side of using academic buildings well up to if not beyond their capacity, a new university may tend to err on the side of keeping the total of its administrative personnel and the total of its administration costs too low. This may also be encouraged by considerations connected with the building programme. Administrators take up space. Space is scarce and the first claims on it should be for academic use. Moreover the first space available in a new university must be

F

space for administrators. They are housed while academics as yet are not, Therefore the administrators may tend not to share in the few accessions of accommodation that accrue in the university's earlier years. Therefore, perhaps, they cannot expand, quite apart from the fact that money will not be allocated to their expansion, because they do not have space into which to expand. They may then find themselves both too few in number for the work that is to be done, and too cramped in attempting to deal with it.

(VI)

I must end by pointing out once again that I have been concerned only in the problems of the new universities as I see them. It does not follow that everyone in these universities spends the whole of his time brooding on these problems, any more than it follows that only the new universities have problems, or that everyone in other universities is unconcerned with problems. Again, I have confined myself to the problems that seem to me either to be special to the new universities or to appear with particular force there. They are not the only problems the new universities have to face: these universities are as much subject as any other academic institutions to (for instance) inter-subject rivalries, or to personal rivalries, or to any of the other troubles to which universities are prone.

The main purpose of this postscript, however, is to mention, although strictly it is outside my terms of reference, that, whatever its problems may be, and whether or not these are greater than the problems of other places, the new university is a place in which the academic who is suited will find much satisfaction. At the least this will be the satisfaction of what some people call 'a challenge'. There is plenty to be done. There is order to be instituted, there is a reputation to be made for the university. There are very unfledged students to guide. But there is more. There is an institution coming into existence. There is an opportunity to participate in influencing its physical shape, its academic standards, the pattern of its constitution, its atmosphere. There is probably a greater possibility of experiment than there is in most other places; and if this is so, then there is the particular responsibility that accompanies it. It is not an easy life, whether for senior or for junior academics, and it is not an easy life for the administrators. But it is, no doubt, not without significance that very few who have experienced it appear to wish to change it: very few appear to wish to move back to the institutions from which they have come, or to move on to similar older institutions. This does not imply anything against these institutions. It simply implies that, without being either better or worse than people in other universities, the people who have elected to work in the new universities have found something there to suit them.

THOUGHTS AFTER ROBBINS

W. H. G. Armytage
Professor of Education
University of Sheffield

The first realistic attempt not only to assess but also to garner more efficiently the academic harvests of tomorrow was made by the late Lord Simon. He also suggested in 1956 that an overall survey should be made of the facilities available. But his proposed instrument—a Royal Comission, was dropped, as too cumbrous. Instead, the Prime Minister appointed a small survey group under Lord Robbins to examine the forward uplands of tertiary education and beyond, and make recommendations for its development. This group's Chindit boldness so riveted everyone's attention that when an even quicker-moving group under Lord Taylor profaned the sacred vigil of 'waiting for Robbins', by issuing a boldly (some might say badly or even hastily) drawn sketch map of what could be done, *The Times*, as the traditional diocesan gazette of the universities, protested. In an editorial on 6 March 1963, entitled 'Paper Universities', it described Lord Taylor's plans as of the 'explosive-expansionist variety' and almost sneered

> everything is to be doubled, or trebled, or quadrupled (it is not clear which) within a term of years (it is not clear how many); a crash programme leads into a ten-year plan (thirteen concurrent plans in fact) . . .

In such 'fairy tale pamphleteering', *The Times* continued,

> we are given a peep at some of the practical dragons in the path but they are banished by the magic formula, 'where there's a will there's a way'.

By contrast, Lord Taylor's reply was studiously rational and deflationary. He proposed that

> the gap between potential entrants and places should be measured annually and that expansion should be planned to meet this need,

and that 'excessive specialization in the sixth form' should be mitigated by widening the avenues of entrance to higher education. He also confessed that 'the virulence of the attack' prompted him to wonder whether he and his colleagues 'had not done better than they knew'.

(I)

Now four years later Taylor, rather than Robbins, seems to have been the route map for university advance since 1963. For Taylor called for forty-five new universities in the next twenty years (and with the polytechnics and already upgraded C.A.T.s we are well on the way to that). Taylor called for more intensive use of buildings for five hours a day, five days a week, ten months in a year (and we are moving that way, too). Taylor suggested the use of part-time teachers to rustle the academic groves (and an ever-increasing number of universities are now doing this, too). Above all Taylor canonized the three concepts of 'critical mass', 'economic siting', and 'upgrading', and these subsume most discussions that have taken place in universities ever since. 'Critical mass' involves a viable unit of from eight to ten thousand students. 'Economic siting' involves flexing the resources of under-privileged areas. 'Upgrading' is to institutions what graduation is to students. It is the law of life to any collective body. It is the progress from umbilical dependence through autochthony to autonomy. It is the way most English universities have grown, by 'winning' rather than being given their Charters. The scope of the Taylor operation was such that a senior Minister of Cabinet rank, assisted by a Secretary of State, was to preside over it. A National University Development

Council was to be set up to prepare a ten year plan; and the U.G.C. was to be made more effective. Indeed regional U.G.C.s were suggested in that particular declaration of intent.

These concepts were not new. Others, including the present writer, had put them forward, years before. Commenting in 1956 on the advancing waves of students that were to flood the universities in the years ahead, an editorial for a now defunct scientific journal, *Research* (October 1956, p. 369) indicated five emergency measures. The first, and least questionable, was to expand the existing universities, a policy which to judge by the discussions at the previous Home Universities Conference, was not being undertaken with the urgency required. The second was to divert some of the flood to upgraded technical colleges (a continuation of the Percy proposals of 1945). The third involved the recognition of work done in certain training colleges as contributing to graduate status (an old chestnut of 'Bruce Truscot').[1] Thus, some of these colleges (once the three-year course was introduced) could be recognized as affiliated institutions and provide courses leading to general science or arts degrees for intending teachers; or certain technical colleges, instead of working for external degrees of the University of London, take internal degrees of their regional university. The fourth, most important, yet most difficult and most questioned, was to found new universities. The issue in February of that year of a memorandum by the Director of Education for Brighton pointing out that a University College of Sussex would provide a complement to the already flourishing college of technology in Brighton, seemed to several a symbol of what might be done to give arts graduates the opportunity to acquire a little more of modern science than that known to an ancient Briton. It also looked like mitigating the desperation with which the older civic universities faced the problem of finding lodgings for

[1] The *nom de guerre* of a distinguished academic whose *Red Brick University* (1943) and *Redbrick and these Vital Days* (1945) were republished as *Red Brick University*, Penguin Books, 1951.

their students. Students in Manchester found it so difficult to compete with young businessmen and technologists offering four or five guineas a week, that they were forced to live further and further away from their universities, and colonies of them grew up as far away as Altrincham, Bramhall and Stockport (*Manchester Guardian*, 7 September 1956). To meet this difficulty it seemed logical to follow the example of the United States and found university 'branches' in town centres needing them. Thus, Birmingham could have a branch at Wolverhampton, and Manchester another at Blackpool. This fifth measure was based on regional density of housing.

Two years later such regional arguments were examined in greater detail by Professor W. G. V. Balchin, who concluded that inhabitants of the expanding economies of southern and eastern England needed ready access to new universities. It was also suggested by Professor (now Sir) Neville Mott that perhaps it would be cheaper to take poets, historians, linguists and philosophers to research complexes like Harwell rather than try to recreate research complexes in a cathedral environment. The argument could, and was, extended. The tendency of arts lecturers to 'go sour' in an academic environment abstracted from the industrial world, led to 'The case for Scunthorpe' (*New Statesman*, 3 March 1961):

> This tang of realism would do the arts no harm. A university in Scunthorpe (or Bolton, Sunderland, Crewe, Derby or Stevenage for that matter) would be more than a mere intellectual cistern, liable to run dry. For the activities in all these towns tap springs of speculation. No don can 'disengage' from such an environment.
> A marriage between the industrial towns and the universities has to take place if the bitter taste of our own industrialization is to be assuaged. The natural recoil at the thought of a university in Scunthorpe stems largely from the basic aversion which Englishmen have to going native.

(II)

The claim of the large cities and centres of population for further facilities for higher education was, as Robbins suggested, taken seriously. So seriously that a new institution of higher education has taken root: the 'polytechnic'.

This was also helped by another Robbins recommendation, that equal performance merited equal academic awards. So it was decided to make degrees available to those doing work of degree standard in institutions with no degree-awarding powers. Their brainchild, the Council for National Academic Awards, began operations in September 1964 with far greater powers than its predecessor, the National Council for Technological Awards. For its mandate was not restricted to technology, nor to sandwich courses, nor limited to England and Wales. Its degrees, comparable in standard to those at present conferred by universities, are increasingly available to both full-time and part-time students at institutions of higher education or research, other than universities, who have undertaken certain approved courses of study or research. In a rare, but unfortunate, euphoric lapse at the Woolwich Polytechnic on 27 April 1965 the Secretary of State for Education and Science described such institutions as comprising, with colleges of education, the public sector of higher education. In fact, in this so-called public sector, the principles of viability and critical mass have been successfully applied, resulting in the creation of a new type of degree-awarding institution—the polytechnic. As defined in circular 11/66 by the Department of Education and Science on 12 April 1966 (*A Plan for Polytechnics and Other Colleges of Higher Education in the Further Education System*, Cmnd. 3006, May 1966), some twenty-seven institutions of high academic standards and with a satisfactory corporate life were to be so designated. Designed to maintain closer and more direct links with industry, business and the professions, they were to enrol part-time as well as full-time teachers and students.

These proposed polytechnics are to develop and expand the public sector, and to fulfil the enlarged target in the National Plan (para. 23, p. 198) of 70,000 full-time and sandwich students by 1969-70, who will follow advanced courses in institutions of further education (as opposed to the target of 51,000 by 1973-4 put forward by the Robbins Committee). They represent the need to concentrate this teaching at a limited number of major centres.

At present some 7,000 students are working for C.N.A.A. degrees, of whom 6,000 are in science and engineering. But it is doubtful whether these will reach 10,000 in the next quinquennium as, at present, such degrees are confined mainly to science and engineering.

When on 5 April 1967 the Minister for Education and Science confirmed that twenty-eight institutions would, as indicated the year before, be raised to the status of poly-technics he placed the coping-stone on the new pluralistic concept of higher education. These twenty-eight, to be supplemented by two more by the end of the year, represent the height of the Department's ambitions. For the next ten years, no more will be added to the list.

In these polytechnics are to be concentrated the degree work for the students studying for the degrees of the Council for National Academic Awards, together with others who want a full-time course which, although not of degree standard, leads to one or other of the many professional qualifications marked by a certificate or an associateship. The work and functions of these polytechnics and of the universities are not to be regarded as mutually exclusive, and it is hoped that there will be considerable co-operation between them. But though these polytechnics will have the maximum autonomy consistent with the responsibilities of the local authority (at least five members of the academic staff as well as the principal will be on the governing body), their degrees will be those of a central body, the Council for National Academic Awards.

Will these polytechnics, like their students, be ultimately able to 'graduate' to university status? The Minister's promise to build these up into crack institutions, virtual replacements for the colleges of advanced technology (which themselves have 'graduated' to university status), led the *Times Educational Supplement* of 7 April 1967 to

> hope straight away that neither the polytechnics nor any one else will imagine that one day they too may be eligible for the university world. Enough, for a long time to come, is enough. At long last we should now be set for a period when we can and must try to sort out the implications of so many major policy changes in so few years and to rethink seriously our philosophy of higher education.

(III)

The first element in any such 'philosophy', as any observer of the United States would agree, should be to discriminate between undergraduate and postgraduate study. Here Robbins uncovered the startling growth in the proportion of graduate to undergraduate students—1:5 in 1961, as opposed to 1:15 in 1939. Nor does this figure include the more sapient sutlers who drift across the Atlantic as their nineteenth century forbears crossed the Rhine. Giessen has its present day counterparts in Berkeley, Indiana, and Ann Arbor. And as the biological and physical sciences grow more political as well as more polyphiloprogenitive the drift increases. 'Drain', with its overtones of contempt, is an unhappy word to use; *hegira* might be better.

Such quaternary education has led to universities being graded, like teams in the football league. But, as in football, the opportunities for first class teams are so small that the drift will continue as a registration of protest. Here another remark of Lord Taylor's is relevant. Protesting against Lord Hailsham's remark in the House of Lords on 27 February 1963 that the American recruiting drive for British scientists was an impressive tribute to the inability of the American high school system to service its own universities and scientific institutions with graduates of the right ability, he wrote that the real reason was insufficient expansion of higher education at home (*The Times*, 25 March 1963).

Here the upgrading of the C.A.T.s, the establishment of polytechnics, and the general adoption of the policy of allowing students at colleges of education to read for degrees might enable universities to delegate to them some courses at the tertiary level. Even before the Labour Government came to power, Dr. Balogh was on record as saying that 'the reform of higher education necessitates much more than an expansion of what is'. The present author also remarked (in *Forum*, 6, 1964, 76) 'as we move into an era where regional responsibilities become ever more important, it is surely necessary to expand teacher training facilities at technical Colleges, colleges of art and similar types of institutions, to enrich recruitment to the profession'.

If the 'untapped potential' revealed by Robbins is to be utilized, new degree structures will be needed, especially for girls. As Robbins showed, their untapped potential is considerable. In 1961, 11,475 girls entered colleges of education as opposed to 4,836 boys, whereas only 7,475 girls entered the universities as opposed to 18,067 boys. Nor do girls enjoy other forms of full-time further education: only 2,039 of them were to be found there as opposed to 8,200 boys. An even greater disparity in part-time education is revealed: only 1,272 girls as opposed to 33,958 boys. Indeed the total figures (22,261 girls as opposed to 65,061 boys) themselves are inadequate, since these 22,261 girls represent 7·1 per cent of their total age group, whereas the 65,061 boys represent 21·3 per cent of their group.

They will obviously form the bulk of candidates for the B.Ed. degree envisaged by Robbins—two academic subjects and Education. This (under pressures of student enrolment and legitimate collegiate ambition) has already become, in some cases, one academic subject and Education, for which the universities, especially during the financial squeeze of 1966, virtually delegated the teaching to the colleges of education. Moreover, Robbins's concept of the universities 'taking over' the colleges of education was neatly sidestepped when colleges secured such rights to teach for the B.Ed. degree (though not themselves awarding it).

Subsequent remarks of the Plowden Committee of 1967 (para. 978) indicate that overall planning of the outlines of courses is essential:

> The degree put forward for consideration in the Robbins Report was envisaged as consisting of Education and two other main subjects. This is well suited to the needs of students for secondary teaching who would be equipped with two strong teaching subjects and a limited range of curriculum courses in other subjects. But students training for primary teaching need a wider range of experience than they will be able to acquire if they have to concentrate on two main subjects and the theory of education.

> We hope that as universities, institutes of education and colleges come into closer contact, ways will be found of reconciling high academic standards in the B.Ed. course with relevance to primary education. We also hope that, as soon as possible, arrangements will be made for B.Ed. courses to be taken by established teachers.

Like the C.N.A.A. degrees, the B.Ed. poses the desirability of universities not so much sharing as shedding some of their tertiary load. But they face the even bigger problem of what to take on. Should they, or even can they, develop postgraduate schools on the American model? Current advice (December 1967) from the U.G.C. indicates that they should not, and that many post graduates should be encouraged to go into industry or teaching. Or are they, as the French planners are, just unable to give figures about this? For though Jean Fourastié confidently assesses that the number of those taking the *baccalauréat* (university entrance requirement) will rise from 49,000 in 1959 to 260,000 in 1975 and 400,000 in 1985, and that those taking the *licence* will rise from 18,000 in 1959 to 70,000 in 1975 and 120,000 in 1985, he is unable to give even a putative figure for doctorates (*Les 40,000 heures*, Paris, 1965, p. 116). In the ultimate reckoning, entry into Europe will bring us face to face with the even more disturbing concept of the *Grande École*.

(IV)

Other days of reckoning are at hand. More than twice the percentage of educational expenditure in the national budget—6 per cent—and more than five times the amount —£37 million—was spent on the universities: some £207 m. between 1955–56 and 1965–66. The auditor is in this case the Committee of Public Accounts which, since 1948, had urged that the Treasury should regularize by statute the *ad hoc* system of university grants and allow the Comptroller and Auditor-General to examine their capital expenditure. Information at present available, it complained in 1950, did not enable a judgement to be made as to whether university grants were administered 'with due regard to economy'. The Treasury itself opposed this pressure as 'getting too near the right in the first place of the Comptroller and Auditor-General and . . . indeed of Parliament itself to go behind the actual grants given to universities and raise questions about or criticize the academic policy of the university which lies behind them' (6th Report, p. 6,471). But the Gater Committee, appointed by the U.G.C. (Cmnd. 9, H.M.S.O., 1956), recommended stricter control of university expenditure. Duly initiated in 1956, yet further steps were recommended by the Rucker Committee (Cmnd. 1235) in 1960.

A 'new examination' was instituted after Robbins, which had strangely Taylorian undertones. Published as the *Fifth Report from the Estimates Committee* (H.M.S.O., 1965), it argued that the country had not yet willed the means for the end it had accepted. More important, it raised the further problem of getting value for money. This, it argued, needed a reorganized University Grants Committee to provide the incentives for efficiency and economy, since the State provides ninety per cent of the capital cost and seventy per cent of the current income of universities. The U.G.C. had already received the message, and set up a working party in March 1965 under its Deputy Chairman to which eight registrars and finance officers were invited.

As a result it was decided to recommend that revised forms of return should be issued for the academic years 1965–66 designed to separate and quantify the cost of undergraduate teaching; the cost of postgraduate work; and the cost of research by university staff. The recommendation was accepted by the U.G.C. and issued to universities.

A second costing exercise, this time between the D.E.S. and the U.G.C., resulted in the institution of a common standard of residential accommodation for universities, C.A.T.s and colleges of education. Based on the 'study-bedroom unit' this uniform scheme applied to all residential schemes programmed to start in 1965 and subsequent years. A third costing exercise is taking place to see if the C.L. A.S.P. system of building schools is adaptable to university science and technology buildings. A fourth aims at establishing 'norms' for equipment allowances for such buildings, especially chemistry and engineering. A fifth, to cope with replacing obsolete scientific equipment, has been undertaken by the D.E.S., the U.G.C., the S.R.C. and the Treasury.

The by now hoary proposal that the Comptroller and Auditor-General should have powers to inspect university accounts was accepted by the Secretary of State for Education and Science in the House of Commons on 26 July 1967. Three months later the Committee of Vice-Chancellors and Principals had a meeting with the Comptroller and Auditor-General. This was on 20 October.

Some vice-chancellors had earlier gone on record as advocates of better 'plant utilization'. Thus, Lord Bowden regarded existing university terms as obsolete survivals from an agricultural era fixed when students had to be released to cope with seed-time and harvest. In the Press (*Sunday Times*, 29 January 1967) he made three points:

1 'Our plant is scandalously under-used'.

2 'We have everything to gain and nothing to lose from the regular assessment of the claims of all those who wish to research'.

3 'The whole policy of student grants might also be examined'.

Lord James had also welcomed the recommendation since he considered it would confirm his belief that the universities 'are more economical and carefully controlled than some other sectors even of the public economy . . . But this has not only got to be true, it must be seen to be true'. He was joined by Mr. C. F. Carter who considered the inspection of university accounts was preliminary to making the case for British universities to be the most efficient and progressive in the world. 'The provision of information for a sovereign Parliament' he considered essential.

Such inspection would do much to alleviate the fears of those who subscribed to what Professor C. H. Waddington described twenty years before in *The Scientific Attitude* (Penguin, 1947, p. 137) as a 'wastage of intellectual ability which no technically competent biologist would tolerate . . . in his rat colony for a week, and a pig business which treated the swine like that would be bankrupt in a couple of seasons'. For Waddington posed the question

> What are universities really training their students for ?
> Are they giving a general education in culture and citizenship, or are they trying to turn out technical experts ? If the former, what are the crucial lessons which can be taught in the different faculties and how are the courses related to getting these lessons across; or, if the latter, what kind of experts, what proportions of the various types of specialists, and so on ?

As the first Chairman of the Central Advisory Council, Sir Fred Clarke, remarked in *Freedom in the Educative Society* (1947), 'developments seem to be moving towards the creation of some kind of Ministry of Culture, not indeed to reduce the natural jungle to a trim totalitarian garden but to minimize wasted effort, to increase effectiveness, and above all to interpret and direct institutional action of whatever kind that has a distant educational bearing so that it may contribute towards the ends of a genuine common culture'.

No one could expect the Robbins Committee to provide an adequate answer to these questions. Yet, by addressing its collective self to them, it has enabled readers to frame different ones, perhaps capable of more definitive answers. Acceptance of its recommendations has been followed by the creation of a new Ministry of Science and Education, which has inherited two major operational techniques already forged by the old Ministry: one concerned with buildings, the other with curricula.

By adopting the key ideas of annual building programmes, minimum physical and educational standards and a limit of costs per place, the old Ministry coped with the bulge cheaply and well. A programme similar to C.L.A.S.P. or S.C.O.L.A. for the universities, based on exterior shells, might well be the answer to crash expansion, allowing interiors, in science at least, to be pulled about by restless professors. More light is needed on the dark corridors linking schools and universities, and the cultivation of basic skills of language and number in ways less esoteric than those now employed.

Unification of the whole service under one Ministry has made possible further data-assembly for forward planning. A consultative structure for higher education in gear with the University Grants Committee, the Central Advisory Council, the Secondary Schools Examinations Council, the National Advisory Council for the Training and Supply of Teachers, and the National Advisory Council on Education for Industry and Commerce will enable targets to be set and operational research insights applied to the whole. To monitor the impact of all this, the now large and cumbrous Committee of Vice-Chancellors and Principals has, as from 1 April 1967, organized itself into a series of small working divisions to tackle problems that need a concerted approach by all universities.

These problems fall under five main heads and the working divisions will keep these under regular review not only to deal expeditiously with them but to foresee future implication and further problems in their fields. Thus,

Division A will be concerned with university development: overall student numbers, capital grants, university building and use of capacity. Division B will cope with recurrent finance, including support for research, the level of fees, the index of university costs and the vexed and difficult problem of cost analysis. Division C will deal with staff and student affairs, salaries, the ratio of staff to students and other concerns under this general head. Division D will be concerned with the relations of universities with other institutions of higher education, government establishments, industry, the schools, exchange schemes and the general ecology of universities at the tertiary and quaternary level. Finally Division E will keep under review relations with universities overseas through such organizations as the Association of Commonwealth Universities, the Association of American Universities, the European Rectors' Conference and other such bodies. The meetings of these divisions will be intercalated with those of the main Vice-Chancellors' Committee, which now meets six times a year.

The advantages of this new divisional structure are fourfold. Firstly, since all Vice-Chancellors will be members of one or another division, it will enable them to gain for themselves more detailed insights into the problems facing them than they have hitherto been able to obtain. Secondly, wider consultation with general university opinion will be possible, for the committee is considering the formation of an academic consultative group to meet them from time to time. As at present envisaged this will involve two or three members of staff being appointed by each university to contribute their expert knowledge on particular topics. Thirdly, the *ad hoc* arrangements for consulting with the University Grants Committee and the Association of University Teachers will now be replaced by regular meetings, and similar arrangements for standing joint committees with industry, heads of schools and local authority associations will be strengthened. The fourth, an inevitable concomitant of all these changes, is the establishment of an intelligence and information officer and of statistical resources to provide the data for many of these working parties.

(V)

The Robbins Committee wanted a grants commission to be created with responsibility for the whole field of higher education. So the matching recommendations of the Trend Committee of enquiry into the organization of civil science (Cmnd. 2171, 1963) led to the U.G.C. being placed under the Minister of State for Civil Science and the Universities. This Ministry was announced as a component of the Department of Education and Science on 6 February 1964. It was to embrace civil science as well as universities, whilst another Minister of State was to be responsible for schools. Both Ministers of State were to be under a single 'overlord' Minister.

Given direct access both to the new Secretary of State and to the two Ministers of State, and reinforced in size (it now numbers 22), the U.G.C. began to issue in 1965 a separate *Annual Survey*. This originated five years earlier as a preface to its annual statistical returns, since the interval between the quinquennial reports was too long in days of such rapid development.

The sheer number of universities has now meant that, from being a 'buffer', the University Grants Committee is to become a signal box. This was admitted by its Chairman on 22 February 1965 to the estimates committee (Fifth Report, question 303, p. 50) when he doubted that existing quinquennial practice was 'practicable in the present shape'. In its place he suggested 'either a three-year period or a six-year period divided into two three-year periods, or a rolling quinquennium'. Either would involve a revision of the visitation policy. This was accepted by the estimates committee which recommended that such changes should be put into effect 'early in the next quinquennium'. But the estimates committee went still further by recommending that the Secretary of State review the composition and responsibilities of the U.G.C. with a view to increasing both its part-time and full-time membership.

More constructive and effective guidance will now be given to universities in planning buildings. Statistical, cost accounting, engineering, and architectural departments are being established within the U.G.C. to enable it to discharge its new role. It is also to 'inaugurate an exercise to work out standard requirements for university buildings', to examine the proposal that contractors tendering for constructing buildings should be asked to tender for their maintenance as well, and to invite the National Buildings Agency, together with experienced contractors, to pool information on industrial building techniques. A survey of 'at least all major scientific departments in universities' to determine the degree of obsolescence in equipment, was also recommended. A formidable group of former university teachers in the House of Commons kept these questions alive. Thus Professor J. P. Mackintosh, M.P., suggested on 5 July 1966 that the U.G.C. should be replaced by a select committee on the lines of that for the nationalized industries.

He was followed, in another place and in another mood, by Lord Robbins himself. At the British Academy on 6 July 1966 the architect-in-chief of the most discussed report of the century on higher education made a case for a strengthened and more responsible U.G.C. to co-ordinate and make policy, and to report more frequently and extensively, to reassure the public that it was doing this. This, he argued, would 'protect academic institutions against the cruder incursions of politics and create an area in which freedom to maintain their own standards and initiate their own development would be reasonably well presented'.

(VI)

Freedom of choice depends on the choices open. Here the multiple or pluralistic concept of tertiary and quaternary education is all to the good, providing it is freely admitted that each type has its own virtues. C.N.A.A. courses might well, by their sandwich nature, facilitate the establishment of more flexible conversion courses for those who feel in need of them, whilst when the 'open university' becomes airborne, it might enable a new pattern to be developed in the extra-mural departments of the civic universities. Some of these, it will be remembered, literally developed from such extra-mural teaching just a century ago.

The next four years, like the last four, will see a continuance of the endless conflict between the forces of order and disorder. Higher education will never be purely functional, since it represents Man's attempt to tune in to tomorrow. Were it anything else, it would be meaningless.

Such freedom is already needed by colleges of education. This the Weaver Report wishes to provide by giving them their own academic boards and independent governing bodies. This was part of the bargain made by the D.E.S. when it rejected the Robbins Committee's proposals that colleges of education should be integral parts of universities, and allowed the Local Education Authorities to maintain their control. No step is more likely to upgrade the colleges in the estimation of the public, since the image of them as being directly under a principal rather than of an academic board still prevails.

Further freedom might well be provided by another D.E.S. circular (10/65), which has undoubtedly accelerated the establishment of comprehensive schools. These schools, when established, might not only delay the harsh vocational choices that are at present being made by children aged 13–15, but also mitigate, by their very size, the crudity of such choices. The crudity, being the result of the limited number of A level combinations at present offered in sixth forms, is best illustrated by the present arts versus science choice.

(VII)

There was nothing really revolutionary about the Robbins Report. Apart from the crisis measures to cope with the bulge it virtually recommended the slowing up of the rate of growth of full-time higher education. The envisaged rate of expansion—5·4 per cent per annum at compound interest —was rather less than that achieved over the previous eight years. If this lower growth is sustained the target figures of 560,000 places for 1980–81 will be reached. Its envisaged annual growth rate in part-time education is lower still— 4·5 per cent per annum—and this has to be continuously sustained to provide 790,000 places by 1980–81 (from 356,000 in 1962–63).

Like all the manpower projections, from Percy, Barlow, Zuckerman, to Willink, this seems to have been another underestimate. Three years after it appeared, student figures at the university were 2,000 above the Robbins projection. Nor was this achieved at the expense of other sectors, which were also well above Robbins estimates. For ever greater proportions of the 747,000 eighteen-year-olds of 1964 and 963,000 of 1965, and the 882,000 of 1966, choose to crowd the institutions of higher education. There were, doubtless, social reasons, folk myths of the sixth form maybe; but in industrial areas the sight of teenage unemployed certainly helped. For these unemployed teenagers had been dislodged from the crumbling cliffs of craft unemployment by the erosive, intrusive kilowatt hour.

The decline of the number of eighteen-year-olds to 724,000 in 1970 will mask this process, but viable structures will have to be set up to cope with the 900,000 of 1980. Such statistical projections, based on the best and most reliable evidence of future needs, are, as Robbins admitted, a continuous need.

Like lemmings, the majority of eighteen-year-olds have been plunging under some compulsive hallucination into the already overcrowded waters of the arts and social sciences, leaving the dry lands of the pure and applied sciences. Failing to obtain places in universities, they do not flock to colleges of education. Instead, they seem to go to the colleges of technology for degrees. The relative status of B.A. (C.N.A.A.) and B.Ed. (university) is already a vexing problem.

The demand for places in the universities rather than the manpower needs of the economy (which were not adequately known) seemed to have been the dominant influence on the Robbins Committee's recommendations. They said that the proportion of the age group obtaining the minimum university entrance qualifications has been rising by 0·37 per cent per year in England, Wales and Scotland. By 1962 it had reached 7 per cent. Assuming the rise would continue, the Robbins Committee estimated it would be 12·9 per cent by 1980, by which time 17 per cent of the age group would be entering full-time higher education. Of these, 380,000 would be in universities. Put in another way, 40 per cent of all entrants to higher education would be in universities by 1980, as opposed to 45 per cent in 1962.

To mediate the demand for places and the opportunities open after graduation, vocational advice, and, more important, future manpower needs are important. So at the London School of Economics a unit for statistical studies was established in association with the Department of Education and Science, to construct a model of the educational system, to ascertain how it may develop over the next twenty-five years, but more important, how it should be developed in the light of national economic targets. Its investigation into the use of qualified manpower in industry, designed to ascertain the relationships between education, job and performance were spread over a hundred firms, beginning with the electrical industry, that great eroder of servile skills.

The wider contours of such plans are to be sketched by the National Economic Development Council. Established in 1962 'to examine the economic performance of the nation with particular concern for plans for the future in both the private and the public sectors of industry', this originally envisaged a growth rate of 4 per cent per annum, based on increased estimates of investment in, amongst other fields, education and housing. In education the most recent forecast (*The National Plan* issued 16 September 1965) envisaged current costs at the universities rising to £159 millions by

1969–70, and capital expenditure in further education rising from £126 millions in 1964–65 to £189,500,000 in 1969–70. Though accepting the Robbins target of 218,000 university places by 1973–74, the plan expected 70,000 places for higher education in technical colleges to be available by the same date. To keep Robbins 'up to date' (amongst other things) a long term planning division has been established in the Department of Education and Science.

Professor John Vaizey in W. Beckerman and Associates, *The British Economy in 1975* (National Institute of Economic and Social Research, Economic and Social Studies XXIII, Cambridge University Press, 1965) anticipates 498,000 places in higher education by 1975 (an advance of 86,000 on Robbins) 77,000 more in universities and 9,000 more in further education. The energy forecasts up to 1975 on which these forecasts were based took no account of North Sea gas, that unpredictable and providential accretion to our resources, which of itself will need yet further echelons of expertise to exploit it.

(VIII)

The erection and expansion of a statistical service has been the greatest contribution of the Robbins Report (*Report*, 73, pp. 255–6, and Appendix Four, Part II). Knowing what is in the pipe-line is essential to any dialogue between the allocators of increasingly scarce national resources and those who are going to expend them. For instance, we now know that arts students in the first year of their sixth form course have increased by 60 per cent from 1962 (26,446) to 1966 (42,339), whilst their coevals studying science had increased by only 20 per cent over the same period (23, 671 in 1962 to 28,295 in 1966). On the other hand, those reading arts/science increased by 106 per cent (from 6,015 in 1962 to 12,339 in 1966). Together, the total number of students from all three groups in the first year of sixth-form study number 82,973, an increase of 48 per cent over the 1962 total of 56,132.

These and other figures now so easily available have led some universities, of which Sheffield is one, to establish Academic Development Committees to monitor such trends, and, in the light of information about the intentions of neighbouring institutions, to plan growth-points for their own institutions. These A.D.C.s also take into account other factors, like the continuing short-fall of suitable candidates for places in departments of applied science. Indeed, a detailed exercise on the institutional anatomy of individual universities would doubtless reveal other adaptative organs which have developed to digest and process such information for the particular institution's well-being. Academic metabolism requires such material as nutriment for sound growth.

(IX)

Watching all this unfold, one cannot throw off a sense of *déjà vu*. To those of us in 1934 who read the conjectural scenario drawn by G. R. Mitchison[1] on the kind of action which would be taken by a 'third Labour Government' (his terminology was pre-war), my foregoing remarks are a kind of preface. For Mitchison not only envisaged the universities being brought 'under the supervision and control of the Secretary for Education' (p. 415), but their connections with professional bodies would be tightened up and strengthened. Oxford and Cambridge were to become 'educational laboratories for the Socialist State', and the 'non-residential universities' were to be 'required to provide what was in effect a university course for public administrators in a Socialist community'.

Much more importantly, however, the machinery of government itself was to be firmly based on six regions (eight

[1] G. R. Mitchison, *The First Workers' Government or New Times for Henry Dubb* London, Victor Gollancz Ltd, 1934. It was described by Sir Stafford Cripps in the introduction as 'the most complete picture of the actual process of the transition to Socialism through democracy that has yet been drawn'.

if Scotland and Wales are included): London and the Home Counties, the Eastern Counties, the West of England, the Industrial Midlands, Yorkshire and the North-East Coast, and Cheshire, Lancashire and the North-West. First run by regional commissioners, and then by elected councils, these regions were to put into effect the National Plan. The commissioners were 'to see that any hostile or dilatory tactics were not allowed to impede' its performance (p. 84). These regional authorities were to be given 'control over all educational revenue and expenditure' in their respective areas 'subject to some exceptions in favour of the universities and one or two other similar institutions' (p. 407).

We are further along that particular road than I have space to trace, but there seems little doubt that Mitchison's scheme together with the Taylor proposals are the relevant milestones along it. The prominent role which the universities are at present playing in the Regional Planning Councils indicates that the next is not far off.

ADVICE TO AN ALDERMAN

James Dundonald

Dear Alderman Rowbotham,

I take it very kindly that you should have read my *Letters to a Vice-Chancellor*,[1] and I am honoured that you now ask my advice about your plans for renewing (or at least keeping alive) the case for establishing a university in your city. I am glad you have not been so shaken by the *fiat* that went forth in February 1965 (no more new universities in England and Wales for the next ten years) that you have put the whole project into deep freeze. Now, indeed, is the time to plan.

Let me begin by saying that if I were writing that book today, six years later, there are several changes in the university scene that I would have to take into account. An outline of the more important of them will be the best background for the advice I have to give. For if anything in the realm of university planning is certain, it is that what looked new and adventurous in 1962 has not always turned out very differently from what had long been unassumingly carried on. So the first step for a University Promotion Board is to ask what is genuinely new in recent university expansion. You will then be able to see what is still needed, and on that basis shape plans which will have the best chance of approval when the time for further development comes.

(I)

You will recall that the original mandate under which the

[1] London (Edward Arnold), 1962. [Ed.]

new universities in this country were brought into being was to make 'innovations in university education'. Reviewing the situation in its early days, the University Grants Committee cheerfully, and perhaps charitably, observed, 'Everywhere we found evidence that universities were regarding the years ahead not merely as a period of physical expansion but also as an opportunity to re-examine their aims and purposes'.[1] There was, unquestionably, a widespread feeling that more was wanted, but not more of the same; and where the University College of North Staffordshire (founded in 1949) had led, the University College of Sussex followed. The original impetus came from a visit to Keele, of which Brighton's Director of Education wrote:

> I am immensely impressed with the enthusiasm and the general aliveness of the corporate body, and I think there is room for another university institution to be established on similar if not identical lines.[2]

Sussex's emulation, at least in curricular terms, took the form of Schools of Study, the grouping together of subjects roughly comparable in scope and working-method; and this pattern was announced as constituting the essential framework elsewhere—for example in the University of Kent at Canterbury and in the University of Essex.[3] Expansion, it rapidly became clear, was going to mean crash-expansion.

[1] *University Development 1957-62* (Cmnd. 2267, Feb. 1964, 240).
[2] Quoted in 'From Keele to Stanmer' by W. H. G. Armytage, *Research* 9 (Oct. 1956), p. 369.
[3] There is, of course, always some danger that 'Schools' will be organized on the basis 'that certain fields should be stuck together, and then, since there [is] no obvious link between them—why, let them be compared' (Andor Gomme, 'Publicity or Promise: the New Universities', in *Delta*, 34 (Autumn 1964), p. 15). Dr. Gomme, who is here tilting against Essex's 'School of Comparative Studies', has a happy phrase to characterize his own university's curriculum. If others (East Anglia, Warwick and Essex) are concerned to arrange undergraduate studies 'in what one of them refers to as a pyramid of progressive specialization' then in the same terms 'Keele's curriculum could be described as a pair of thinnish squat towers on a very wide shallow plinth' (p. 13).

One sign of the haste to get under way was the abandonment both of the old system of initial dependence on London University, and the new system (pioneered by Keele) of tutelage under an 'Academic Council' drawn from a number of universities. The University College at Brighton became the University of Sussex before it opened its doors to students; and it set another precedent in awarding honorary degrees before it could confer real ones. Trend-setting, indeed, became the mark of the new universities; and trumpet-blowing has been its inevitable accompaniment. Perhaps the extreme was reached when the Vice-Chancellor of one new university observed blandly that he and his colleagues were less concerned with being a new university than with being a university. So much for 'innovations in university education'. The short point is that for all the advertising of 'schools' and similar combinative arrangements there is little to be observed that is genuinely original, by which I mean a consistent and constructive attempt to re-think 'subjects' as they have been traditionally delivered to us. When 'Curriculum and Teaching' came up for discussion at a conference of the new universities there was, predictably, 'unanimity of view that every new university must be experimental'; but little else of a substantial kind.[1] (There was of course the ritual chanting of the slogan 'Seminars Good, Lectures Bad'.) We can be sure of one thing: where the innovatory course—timid or adventurous, it makes no matter—is placed as an equal competitor with the orthodox offering, then orthodoxy will win every time. It is not only Vice-Chancellors and their academic colleagues who are ready to identify being a university with being like existing universities. The young have an eye for the prudential choice, too. If one thing stands out a mile from the contemporary scene it is that combinative studies, 'integrated' courses, cross-fertilization courses—call them by whatever name you like—will not stand a chance unless they are so

[1] C. I. C. Bosanquet and A. S. Hall, *The Creation of New Universities*, based on a Conference at the University of Keele, 14–16 July 1964, p. 10.

H

firmly written into the university's statement of its aims that they cannot become a side-show or peripheral circus, but are plainly seen to be the university's central concern and, as such, requiring participation from all its teachers. What is essential is a distinctive programme which is not window-dressing or pious affirmation but which requires in every teaching member of the university a willingness to re-think his subject and to re-examine the possibilities of teaching it. For only by this means does a university have any coherent attraction for its members, aside from the accidents of traditional prestige or the standing of particular departments. The point is of overriding importance and I shall come back to it. For the moment, I would say with all possible emphasis that you must continue to plan a course of studies that will require this kind of exertion from your teaching staff. 'Innovation' isn't over yet; not by a long chalk.

(II)

The kind of change which, writing five years ago, I had least reason to expect was the sort of financial control that suddenly came above ground in December, 1966, when Mr. Crosland made sure that the fees for overseas students would rise by announcing that the sums which would sustain them at their existing level would not be forthcoming. You could charge your overseas students what you liked—provided the money came out of your own pocket. It is to the credit of the Committee of Vice-Chancellors and Principals that they expressed opposition not only to the effect of the government's measure, but to its being made without prior consultation with the universities, a clear contravention of established practice. There is in this a deep-seated danger, on which the Principal of London University focused attention.[1] Financial control, as mediated through the University Grants Committee, has been wholly necessary and, on the whole, enlightened in its operation.

[1] *The Times*, 11 May 1967.

But access by the Comptroller and Auditor-General to university accounts is bound to be very different in its approach and methods. The real threat in all this is, as Sir Douglas points out, a disturbance of the balance of power within universities. Hitherto, in our system—as sharply distinct from the American—the university teachers have been the important body. Administration has been there to serve a single purpose—to put teacher and student together with a minimum of fuss, and to leave them to get on with their work, that work being the university's essential *raison d'être*. Everyone who has any experience of the American scene knows the tension between 'administration' and 'faculty', ranging from cheerful recrimination to implacable hostility: and everyone who meets it for the first time marvels how it came about, and why the American academic accepts it as a law of nature. Well, it's in prospect for us now; and the solidification of 'administration', with its accounts impeccably ready for the Auditor-General's green ink, is reinforced, as Sir Douglas observes, by the growth of a professional class of university administrators where formerly there were, in the senior ranks at least, only academics who had developed an administrative capacity. I am no friend to the tradition of the amateur, least of all the gentleman amateur.[1] Too many academics, I readily admit, find their way into administration because they have no special gift of any kind, including an administrative gift. All the more reason to see what can be done to prevent a further division of energy into a split between 'administrators' and 'academics'. There are, I believe, some measures which can be brought into the forefront of planning.

We might begin with some observations which the Warden of All Souls quotes—dare one say?—with relish from Mark Pattison's *Memoirs:*

> The men of middle age seem, after they reach thirty-five or forty, to be struck with an intellectual palsy, and

[1] See *Letters to a Vice-Chancellor*, p. 36.

betake themselves, no longer to port, but to the frippery work of attending boards and negotiating some phantom of legislation with all the importance of a cabinet council —*belli simulacra cientes*. Then they give each other dinners, where they assemble again with the comfortable assurance that they have earned their evening relaxation by the fatigues of the morning's committee. These are the leading men of our university, and who give the tone to it—a tone as of a lively municipal borough . . .[1]

'A lively municipal borough', indeed: though I doubt whether any borough council is so lively as to have its membership wholly made up of people who are trained to see all sides of a question and who do not scruple to give the last speaker, whose views they oppose, a couple of arguments he hadn't thought of. That kind of liveliness is of course a form of death; and the pity is that academics are an unconscionable time dying. An acceptance of prolonged and inconclusive debate lies, I think, at the root of so much that is wrong in our universities. From it, the best minds escape. The 'brain-drain' undoubtedly draws many who are sick of the deliberative assemblies to which their own time, and the fate of their departments, is irrevocably committed. There is a strong attraction in the common North American pattern of an authoritative administration which is the source of all major decisions, signs all contracts, and is there to listen to sense, not circuitous nonsense. The practice of rhetoric, we are told, grew up in the Greek Commonwealth through the necessity of every man being able to speak in his own cause at need. Perhaps that kind of end-product would be worth the enforced tedium of committee, Senate and Council. But as it is, the university politician is an unpersuasive speaker, holding forth in his own cause and anyone else's, as the fancy takes him, with or without need.

[1] John Sparrow, *Mark Pattison and the Idea of a University*, Cambridge, 1967, p. 120. Lucretius's words may, in this context, suggest a sufficient explanation of the ardours (and the well-drilled simplifications) of the Senate's phantasmal warfare—that it is a retreat from the university's real, though complex, cares and concerns.

To leave this for service under an authoritarian administration is, of course, simply to exchange one set of problems
for another. But the change itself may be overpoweringly
attractive when 'the fatigues of the morning's committee'
and 'the tone as of a lively municipal borough' have stifled
initiative and brought necessary development to a dead-
end. Those who have known the system longest are least
able to find words for the aggregate waste of time, the re-
working of old, old issues, the 'intellectual palsy' which is
only diagnosed when it is all but incurable.

The real danger in this is not so much any losses through
the 'brain-drain' (which is by no means the one-way current
its name would suggest) but the growing distance between
the professor, head of his department and watchdog of its
interests on all the committees and bodies of which he is
ex officio a member, and the people he has to teach. The
saying Clark Kerr quotes, concerning the faculty member
in the American context, is increasingly true here—'The
higher a man's standing, the less he has to do with students':
and a further widening of the gap is made by those sources
of additional income which have given rise to 'the affluent
professor'. Do we recognize anything of our own situation
in this description of professorial life ? :

> a rat race of business and activity, managing contracts
> and projects, guiding teams and assistants, bossing crews
> of technicians, making numerous trips, sitting on com-
> mittees for government agencies, and engaging in other
> distractions necessary to keep the whole frenetic business
> from collapse.[1]

True, British professors are, on the whole, bound rather
more closely to the wheel of their own university's committees; so that our system, though similarly self-perpetuat-

[1] Quoted in 'Can the liberal university survive ?' by W. H. C. Eddy
in *The Australian Highway*, 47 (March 1967), p. 6. (Mr. Eddy's
immediate source is Clark Kerr's *Selections from 'The Uses of the
University'*.)

ing, is comatose rather than frenetic. But the essential characteristic remains—a rapidly growing distance from the activity of advancing and disseminating knowledge, which increasingly tends to be thought of (with real or pretended regret) as 'something I was once allowed to get on with'.

Against this background it is easy to see, and to a large extent to sympathize with, the move towards 'student power'. The Vice-Chancellor of Manchester University has pointed out that students can be adversely affected when those who should be teaching them are working for industrial or other extraneous bodies. In one year, he computes, there were 160 instances of leave of absence, 'many for a few days but some for a term or a year'.[1] As to that, one can only hope that any university, not Manchester alone, will have a closer eye to limiting the one-or-two days' absence while putting on a firmer basis the arrangements for regular periods of study leave. The principle of 'sabbatical leave' is all too often, in British universities, honoured in principle and neglected in practice; and few things are so necessary, as a bedrock condition of service at whatever academic rank, than clear entitlement to leave of absence. Nothing can finally prevent a university dying in its own circle of futile debate—adrift, as in a never-to-be forgotten Marx Brothers last scene, on a wide and empty ocean, intent to the last on its own beautiful music. Still, the opportunity of knowing by direct contact what is happening elsewhere—by revisiting the field of one's own scholarship as well as by travelling to other universities—will ensure that some at least of those on board can recognize the signals and will speak up when the fatal drift sets in.

If it is important to check any tendency to regard the teaching of students as a secondary activity, it is above all necessary to stop undergraduate students from being thought of as making less demand than the postgraduates. 'Any fool', they used to say north of the Tweed, 'can take the Honours students: it needs a good man to teach the

[1] *The Times*, 18 May 1967.

Ordinary class'. I am sure this is true; and equally sure that it is a truth of real and lasting benefit to the teacher as well as his students. Until a teacher has had to re-think his subject, through the necessity of presenting it to an intelligent but unspecialized audience, there is a sense in which he remains the victim of that subject—its heredity and environment are binding upon him, for they go without close examination. We have all met learned men who, by remaining always in the orbit of their specialism, have illustrated exactly Bernard Shaw's dictum upon the ignorant —the more ignorant, the more convinced 'that their little parish and their little chapel is an apex to which civilization and philosophy have painfully struggled up'. If a man is under no *practical* necessity of asking what is essential and what is marginal in his professional activity, he is likely to take as normal and natural what may be provisional and accidental. How should he know any better, except by having to view the activity from the standpoint of uninformed curiosity? Here, again, the argument for a common core of studies seems to me decisive. It confronts the teacher inescapably with what he claims to know, his 'subject'; and it puts him in a living relationship with his students, the undergraduates chief among them.

One other aspect of 'student power' deserves notice. It was evident at the London School of Economics that the split was not simply between teachers and taught: it was also between teachers and teachers. One estimate puts the number of staff members who 'joined meetings which were highly critical of authority's actions and sympathetic to the students' complaints' as high as 80.[1] There are always, of course, those hapless figures who strike that least demanding of all academic postures, falling over backwards. My own favourite would be the Professor of Sociology who helpfully explained to the readers of the *Daily Telegraph* that

the value of a university education is not derived from slavishly attending lectures or reading books, but also

[1] *The Times*, 29 March 1967.

from talking with fellow-students (or anybody else) over coffee, drinks, in the streets, in your rooms at night and also in spending a good deal of time alone—thinking.[1]

Tell *that* to Mark Pattison. Would it perhaps dispel his fear that 'Public Opinion, not dissatisfied at the degradation of a University into a School, is disposed still further to lower the level of instruction' ?[2] Or does the ban on slavish attendance at lectures—and on reading 'books': should they be reading (non-slavishly, of course) learned journals, or the newspapers ?—does this suggest rather the fulfilment of fears Pattison once entertained for the lecture 'as an instrument', so Mr. Sparrow puts it, 'of the higher education' ? For non-slavish attendance may well mean

a miscellaneous audience of ladies and gentlemen who come and go during the hour, and who manifest by frequent applause their gratification at the intellectual treat they are enjoying.[3]

The Professor is, of course, doing his best to safeguard readers of the *Daily Telegraph* from supposing that 'a university education' is 'by any means a nine-to-five grind over paperwork'. Believing that his cause is necessary, he stands as a self-appointed mediator. Does not this suggest that he is one of the first to capitulate to a line-up, students versus their bosses, which is essential to the cruder manifestations of 'student power' ?—students 'as a new intellectual proletariat . . . bent on bullying their teachers to act like employers'.[4] The leaders of the National Union of Students behaved with marked good sense throughout the London School of Economics troubles. But the N.U.S. has, inevitably, some of the characteristics of a 'union' in the Trade Union sense; and it is perhaps natural that authority under pressure should attempt to keep the situation in hand by

[1] 'How fair are students to those who foot the bill ?', *Daily Telegraph*, 5 May 1967.

[2] *Mark Pattison and the Idea of a University*, p. 118.

[3] *Ibid.*, p. 132.

[4] *Daily Telegraph*, 18 March 1967.

doing deals with the N.U.S. representatives. This involves, willy-nilly, the university authorities taking up the posture of employers, requiring conditions of work and with-holding areas of participation in joint management. But that this is all a fiction is apparent once either party asks 'Striking against whom ?' At the end of the line, as several commenta-tors have been quick to point out, is a hostile public reaction. There need not be any mistake about the seriousness of the situation. There is a kind of mass hysteria which unites 'Red Guards' (was there ever a more misleading description of children and early adolescents ?), Provos, and students from Berkeley to Buenos Aires—a sort of Gadarene syn-drome. Universities are peculiarly theoretical places; the invention of an employer locked in continuous struggles with his workers is not less dangerous because it is inherently absurd.

The scale of our own troubles is small. A share in the government of the university is a natural step, and one already taken in a fair proportion of the newer institutions. A greater emphasis on the university teacher's prime responsibility to his students is the more important, because longer-term, consideration. I have suggested more than once that it is only through a central programme of studies, explicitly the common concern of all departments in the university and expressly the responsibility of its professors, that the real balance will be restored and maintained. It is time to specify what is meant.

(III)

As I said in 1962, attempts to interrelate the subjects taught in a university can most conveniently be regarded under two main heads. There is, firstly, the grouping of the curriculum into major subjects (those on which the student is going to spend most of his time) and minor ones (those he is going to pursue in less depth, and often with a design of intellectual support or practical utility in relation to the major subjects). Such a curriculum-grouping may be in terms of 'schools of study' (largely determining the choice and relation of the major subjects, but often having some bearing on the minor ones), or it may be more loosely answerable to certain principles of combination which can affect both major and minor subjects. An example of this latter kind is Keele's line-up of all subjects into three group-ings—arts, social sciences, experimental sciences—with the student being required to take two majors (studied for three years at a time) and two minors (studied for a year, usually both together in the first year of degree-work), always subject to the provision that every predominantly arts or social sciences course shall include an experimental science minor (or 'subsidiary' as Keele calls them), and, of course, vice-versa.

So much for the first kind of interrelation. The second kind consists of attempts to provide a 'humanizing' influence which will counteract the separate specialisms of the degree-course. It is here that a deep-rooted assumption comes to light—belief that a general dose of philosophy, or 'great books', or (more fashionably) history of science, will provide a meeting-place for minds otherwise virtually isolated from each other. The ways in which this humanizing can be attempted vary from making it the material of a compulsory first ('Foundation') year, at Keele, to the loose and widely permissive character of York's 'open courses'; and, within both systems, a good deal of utilitarian concern can be al-lowed to influence choice—a language can be learnt from scratch, a subject brought into focus for its 'tool' value, a deal of rust chipped away from schoolboy knowledge of a subject, and so on.

I have argued elsewhere[1] against the general acceptability of a vestibular year. Its gains are many, in particular by providing a view of knowledge while postponing the necessity of specialist choice. Its drawbacks, to my mind, tell decisively against it—above all, the great disservice of presenting highly mature accounts of complex matters to an audience which, standing as it does on the threshold of

[1] *Letters to a Vice-Chancellor*, pp. 89–92.

its university career, is least capable of distinguishing between statement of fact and value-judgement. Such a system runs the risk of debauching curiosity at the outset: and that is too grave a risk to be acceptable. Again, I believe that the long-standing prescriptions for general or humanizing studies are sadly overrated. A dose of philosophy all round will help some to a new stock-taking of what they know, or think there is to be known. But they will be few: unless the course is largely historical and descriptive, it will fail to make any sense at all to the majority; and once it is descriptive it will be fatally external. 'Great Books', again, are almost by definition books least of all amenable to paraphrase and discursive exposition. 'Let no one *tell* you what is in *The Critique of Pure Reason*' is still the truest thing ever said in that line: and it makes no matter whether the 'great book' is philosophy, science, or fiction. It must be encountered on its own terms, or it will lie forever on the farther side of the helpful digest the teacher has made of it. As to history of science, that, I take it, is the biggest illusion of all. What kind of 'history' can we make when the audience has no practical acquaintance with the phenomena we are trying to place in a connected account—the starting-point of a particular scientist, his tacit assumptions, his working-methods, and his capacity to attend to the evidence as it is and not as he thought it must be ? We can certainly welcome any shift from trying to make everyone (in an unexplained sense) literate, to an attempt at giving everyone some sense of an external world which prompts curiosity and remains opaque to preconception. But to bring this about to any effective extent—enough to reinforce in the teachers a sense of discovery—we must teach science, not the history of science; just as to bring the young to any capacity for doubting the pictured solidity of that external world we have to teach not the history of philosophy, but philosophy itself.

My prescription for general or common-core studies would, then, be threefold. Firstly, it should not dominate the beginning of the student's career. Let the student enter upon his chosen field of study and the common-core work at one and the same time; and let common-core work continue throughout the whole course for the first degree, culminating in a thesis which specifically tackles the relation of the common-core studies to the student's own specialized work. In that way, we should begin to have some notion of the actual relations between the two; there would be an end of pious evasion about the meeting-place of the two kinds of study being (somewhere) 'in the student's mind'; and we could hope for a longer-term product in fruitful cross-border studies in the postgraduate field. One of the striking things, I am told, about interrelation at Keele is that, as external examiners have been heard plaintively to murmur, there is little evidence in the finals scripts of the other 'principal' subject. It is greatly to Keele's credit that they, alone, of the new universities require a crossing of the Snow-line (the student majoring in arts being required to take a minor in science and vice versa); and I can well believe that in planning and in execution the minors or 'subsidiaries' of this kind (a one-year look at science for the highly trained arts man, and so on) are among the most exciting courses in the university. But the real scope for interrelation has been missed once the common studies are confined to, and are the sole concern of, the first year—a year which, since it forms no part of the degree-course proper, may be felt by the students as less an absorbing preliminary than an increasingly formidable barrier. It is a long trial for young love: and after it the housekeeping of degree work is hard indeed, with too little room for genuine curiosity and no time at all for intellectual diversion. 'We've done the wider-oneness bit': now time presses. A tragi-comedy, isn't it? Benevolent omnipotence plans for range and variety and at the same time banishes real freedom of opportunity for a twelve-month. But in this tragi-comedy the exile rarely returns to claim his dukedom; he is too busy with the plantation of his isle for the following three years.

My second consideration is that any programme of common-core work should have its centre in the sciences rather than the arts; and here we can learn from recent intellectual history. C. P. Snow has reminded us that the heroic age of physics was only just beginning when most people thought the subject 'effectively finished'; and, contrariwise, that in late-nineteenth-century biology 'everyone was waiting hopefully for the revelations which actually arrived sixty or seventy years later'.[1] I would place the centre of common-core studies in the easiest of the sciences to approach, the one which potentially comprehends the widest area of human activity, and the one in which, I would argue, co-operation between widely-differing specialisms is outstandingly necessary to any distinctive advance. This is the claim I would make for a common core of studies to be designated Life Sciences, having at its centre a school of biology and zoology, and in its planned scope the fields of anthropology and human geography, sociology and ethnology, psychology and the creative arts.

A tall order? Let's take it step by step. Entry to the school would be during the student's first term, and would in the first instance be in terms of a common lecture course supplemented by seminar and laboratory classes varied in membership according to A level specialization. The lecture course should be a simple introduction to man's physical context, starting with an account of the solar system as a setting for the planet Earth, and then treating the emergence of life and the creature Man. The lecture course would be consolidated by two further activities: laboratory work and a weekly seminar. Both of these should be run in two divisions —for those with a predominantly arts and those with a predominantly science background—but the aim should be the same: to uncover the tacit assumptions, sophisticated or naïve, which each group brings to certain fundamental activities. I would take as a starting-point the notion of physical 'laws', and examine the nature of generalization from observed phenomena, by way of the limits of that observation; by this means shaping an elementary critique of man the observer. The nature of the experimental work

[1] *Variety of Men*, London, 1967, pp. 54-5.

would of course vary greatly in depth as between the two groups: for the non-scientists it would constitute an introduction to notions of measurement, mass, and some criteria of reliable statement in relation to time and 'space'. The scientists could have a unique chance of investigating fundamental concepts, which they will hitherto have had to take on trust, in orthodox science teaching, through the pressure to accommodate in school syllabuses a constant proliferation of specialisms. As to the seminars, I would hope for the greatest gain where they were run jointly—by, say (at this stage), a philosopher and a physicist, guiding the attempt (and themselves learning in the process) to think through to some reliable working concepts.

In the second term, and (as before and throughout) concurrently with the student's degree work, the lecture course would remain a common course, and have as its theme the ecology of man and the behavioural characteristics of the primates. The laboratory work would now aim (again for scientists and non-scientists, separately grouped) at uncovering tacit assumptions about what is meant by 'living' things, at exploring the kinds of observation and measurement appropriate to this field, and at some prising-open of vestigial notions of 'evolution'. In the seminars man as an observer of life could be the primary theme, and the questions that would naturally arise (again, under joint seminar-management) would reflect man's distinctive capabilities and limitations as an observer-participant, and the potentialities inherent in purposeful control over environment. That would be enough for the two terms. Let the third term be occupied by the degree work; though it might also see the first shaping of an essay to be written in the long vacation, dealing with an aspect of common-core studies related to the individual student's own degree work —the first point of close contact between the two, and the beginning, if all goes well, of interaction and, in the long run, of positive contribution to cross-border studies.

The same sort of development, in principle, could occupy three terms of the second year and two terms of the final year—with this important difference: that after the first year the lectures would cease to be a single common course, and would in the second and third years be constituted as lecture courses related to the main degree groupings, arts (including creative arts); experimental sciences; social studies. The appropriate common-core lecture courses would be, respectively, life-science (man studied ecologically); psychology and certain areas of communication-theory (man as a perceiver of events and a finder of 'selves', including selves in fictive and mimetic form); and those areas of anthropology and sociology which would sustain a close treatment of man as 'a social animal'. The student would attend one of these lecture courses; but the one he would normally be required to attend would be one of the two farthest from his own main area of study: that is, the student whose degree work lay in the experimental sciences would take either the psychology-communication or the anthropology-sociology grouping; the man specializing in the arts, either the life-science or the anthropology-sociology option; and so on. The seminar and (where appropriate) laboratory work would of course not need to be diversified, once the lecture courses were varied in these ways, since the students frequenting each of the three courses would be relatively homogeneous. At this advanced stage seminars could really tackle rewarding subjects. For example, in the sciences the seminar would be equipped to follow the 'beautiful and subtle' arguments contained in Bohr's *Discussion on Epistemological Problems* and Einstein's *Reply*, as an outstanding—perhaps unique—instance of profitable debate. 'If two men are going to disagree, on the subject of most ultimate concern to them both, then that is the way to do it'.[1] Joint conduct of the seminars would still be highly desirable; and I would require an essay in each of the second and third years, as tangible proof of actual participation, of the student's own growing mastery of an aspect of his specialized studies constructively related to the common-core programme. Perhaps the essay-system would work

[1] *Variety of Men*, p. 83.

best if the three essays were progressive explorations of one theme. Or there may be something to be said for leaving it in a permissive state, at least to start with—that is, the second essay might conceivably tackle a wholly different topic from the first and so allow for any false starts: though I would hope that the third would ordinarily extend and deepen the second. A refinement of the whole scheme might be to have each student a member of a discussion group, deliberately assorted in terms of specialized interests, meeting say once a fortnight for across-the-board discussion, again under joint chairmanship—this time, perhaps, a triple chairmanship drawn from each of the three major divisions, arts, social studies, experimental sciences. Such a system, I am told, works well at Keele during the Foundation year. We could hope to do even better, since our common-core work would keep pace with the student's development throughout his whole career.

(IV)

Such a programme would, I believe, do the greatest good where it matters most—to the teachers. The morale of a university is the morale of its academic staff. But just to ensure that staleness doesn't too easily settle in, there are a few other provisions you can make, though they will depend on the willingness of other universities to put them into effect. It seems plain that, without any large-scale increase in universities beyond the present numbers more and more people are going to live out their working lives in the university of first, or possibly second, appointment. There is no sure safeguard against ossification. But I would like to see at least one university trying its hand at a circuit system, the exchange of teachers, particularly senior ones, within the United Kingdom universities. There is no need to go abroad to feel the challenge of a new audience, or to receive the benefits of a new mind in your midst. It's the best thing in the world for Dr. A to teach for a term in a university he otherwise knows only from the outside. There he will meet colleagues and students delightfully different from those he has left: though oddly enough, Professor B will be saying the same things about Dr. A's department compared with his own. Could we take this even a stage further? One of the least happy features of a protected profession—one in which it is almost impossible to be fired, least of all for incompetence—is the number of people who simply die on the job. They have had their fill of their present university: but how to go elsewhere, in our largely static situation?—unless they are genuine stars and know they are in demand elsewhere. Why not consider some of the advantages of a university service, in which, as in the armed forces, the academic who wished could quickly apply for posting (and cross-posting, if need be)? What about the advantages of a career built in these terms—that is, varying periods of service in universities of different kinds? I know there will be cries of outrage at the notion of 'regimentation'. I also know of the unspectacular but solid good such a system—not as a condition of service, but as a possible form of such service—could do. Most university teachers lead stunted professional lives, painfully limited to their own (and often their own initial) experience. That, or the assiduous globe-trotters; there is no real range. Nor is this confined to the so-called 'provincial' universities, old or new. Powicke, I seem to remember, on coming to Oxford from Manchester, was loftily congratulated on his success in escaping from a provincial university. 'Yes', he murmured thoughtfully, 'to come to a parochial one'. So professors on circuit, and recourse at need to a network of postings and attachments within the university system, may have a useful part to play. I once advocated 'Parkinson's p.s.c.' for would-be administrators.[1] The parallel seems complete.

As to the younger teachers, you are likely to find no shortage of gifted postgraduate researchers; and among them, with ordinary luck, a fair supply of those who can teach—though contemporary cults of the inarticulate are, as it happens, reducing your chances in the arts and social

[1] *Letters to a Vice-Chancellor*, pp. 41–3.

studies fields. You will undoubtedly find people who can expound their subject up to a certain level; but among them are many who have difficulty in taking it any farther except in terms of an opaque craft-jargon. Here the co-chairing of inter-subject seminars will be of the greatest help. But an old-fashioned remedy comes very much to the purpose. I would revive the reading-party, the ten or dozen students meeting under the loose presidency of a faculty member or two during a pre-arranged ten days or fortnight, at a quiet venue. Some of the new colleges of education are almost ideally placed for this role, and would have good reasons of their own to welcome undergraduate reading-parties: and Local Education Authority grants are more readily forth-coming for approved courses of this nature than they were, say, five years ago. The one thing you can't rely upon in your younger teachers (they may or may not have it, but you can't confidently expect it) is any pastoral sense—the notion, even in rudimentary form, that the university teacher's work extends outside the formal engagements of the laboratory and the class-room. This is not laziness, but diffidence, a direct effect of the gap between 'them' and 'us' which characterizes a society fundamentally unsure of itself and inherently suspicious of all forms of authority. In the relaxed and informal conditions of a reading-party each party can discover what in fact it has to give the other: and, so far as the teachers are concerned, this means a chance for those who have a vocation in these terms to discover and extend it.

The profession of university teacher is altering fast. Take my word for it: in another five years you will find four-term years, maximum use of the 'plant', and the conception, to borrow a Californian term, of 'fully employed personnel', based on set proportions of a twelve-month year. The young teachers are not going to resist change. For one thing, they know no better; for another, they are busy trying to read, teach, and advance their subject; and they have, in common with most educated people in Western society today, the strongest sense of guilt about what they take to be 'privilege'. We must do what we can to provide and safeguard conditions in which they can discover their gifts and find full scope for them. The really big change that overshadows all others is this. In the past, British universities have, on the whole, kept the standard of the first degree pretty level. Give or take a point, here or there— this place's English, that other's physics, and so on—what the title B.A. connoted was reasonably consistent, whatever the university conferring it. Much of this was due to the great virtue that whoever taught a subject, even in the smallest places, wasn't the sole judge of proficiency in it. That responsibility lay with a board of examiners, not with a single faculty member who was at one and the same time the authority on his course and the undisputed giver of grades to his students. This, I am afraid, is beginning to crumble, as departments have increasingly to accommodate new specialisms—so that the corps of departmental teachers tends to become a collection of experts in strictly limited aspects of their subject. Here, again, interdisciplinary courses may give valuable if unspectacular help. But the real change is that we are beginning to see something much more like stratification by overall quality. Our universities were once much of a muchness in standards. They are already beginning to show significant variations in quality— the measure of their seriousness of purpose, seen in particular (given our tradition) in the status they accord the undergraduate curriculum, and the reality (as distinct from the window-dressing) of their attempts to reinvigorate it. At present, the stratification looks like being by groups;[1] but it is a fair guess that some parts of what now seem solid groupings will become more distinctly individualized, for better or for worse. One remembers the account given

[1] Everyone can fashion his own. A possible list would run: old provincial (e.g. Manchester, Bristol); emancipated redbrick (e.g. Nottingham, Southampton); old-style new universities (Sussex, York); new-style new (Warwick, Essex); with Keele (insistent on four years, three-quarters residence, and small numbers) as a gallant loner— Oxbridge, in this as in all else, being excepted.

by Evelyn Waugh's GARGOYLE AND STRING of the diversity of private schools: excellent school, outstanding school, first class school, very good school, good school, and—school; which 'frankly', was pretty bad. Will 'university' in its turn come to be pretty bad? There would be a special irony in its doing so. The last decade has heard much talk of up-grading. Colleges of advanced technology and colleges of education have been upgraded, so that they now confer degrees—a leading instance, it may be thought, 'of the ingenuous British habit of believing that you can alter the nature or the value of things by changing their names'.[1] Shall we, in the next decade, see some virtual down-grading among universities? As it stands, ours is, as the *Times* educational correspondent once observed, a 'scattered investment in comparatively small institutions . . . our weakness . . . is dispersal and too many commitments'. There is only one solution, if we wish to maintain one or two first-class (by which we can only mean world-class) institutions: 'they will be maintained, if at all, at the expense of the others'.[2] Abolition is unlikely; down-grading highly probable, perhaps into that category of university which, when the politically-inspired rush to comprehensivise secondary education is over, will be left with the duty of providing four-year courses in which the first year will 'have to be devoted to teaching, at greater expense, work which is now covered in sixth forms'.[3]

(V)

So there you are. I have put all my emphasis on planning for a university which is distinctive—which aims at doing something to keep the pattern of knowledge under con-sistent scrutiny, and in doing that can sustain a way of life

[1] *Mark Pattison and the Idea of a University*, p. 140. Unseemly haste to be first with the B. Ed. degree drew, in one place, the melan-choly reproof, 'We have made our B. Ed. and now we must lie about it'.

[2] *The Times*, 6 May 1967.

[3] *Ibid.*, 3 June (letter from the Vice-Chancellor of Liverpool Uni-versity and others).

JAMES DUNDONALD

challenging for teachers and students alike. Today the whole question of standards is under a double attack: openly, from those who maintain that 'standards must be shaped to the people rather than the people to the standards',[1] covertly from those who dress the windows of the closed shops of unexamined orthodoxy. I wish I could give you some confidence in the outcome for the universities of this country. The L.C.M. society is likely to be reflected, all too faithfully, in the L.C.M. university. Mere size, of course, does not make the crucial difference; the 'multi-university', as Robert Hutchins terms it, 'is not merely a non-university, a pseudo-university: it is an anti-university'. In these terms, there is nothing to choose between the multi-university and the mini-university. Each is the home, not of 'lost causes, and forsaken beliefs, and unpopular names, and impossible loyalties', but of an unremitting concern 'to meet miscellaneous, immediate, low-level needs'. It fosters no noble illusions—only the illusion that it is 'grappling with real problems'.[2] When a number of Vice-Chancellors wrote the cautiously worded letter from which I quoted at the end of the last section, expressing their well-grounded fears for the continuity of sixth form teaching, some Government supporters were reported to be thinking of them as 'acting in concert and flexing their muscles for a direct confrontation with the Government'.[3] There we go again. The tussle worker-students versus employer-professors is repeated at the next echelon. But what do you make of the M.P. who asked 'Who do they think they are?' Heaven help them, they are Vice-Chancellors; and if they have any duty at all it is to open their mouths on issues like these. Society gets the universities it deserves. Can we be content if at the end of the day our universities are in a fair way to satisfy mini-minded demand for the multi-university?

[1] Quoted in *Mark Pattison and the Idea of a University*, p. 147.
[2] *The Times*, 20 March 1967 (report of an address by Dr. Hutchins to a convocation held in New York).
[3] *The Times*, 5 June 1967.

The more reason, then, for your University Promotion Committee to continue its planning. What seemed shadow-boxing only ten years ago is now drawing blood. None of us can find a sufficient reason for standing on the side-lines. When the present bidding and counter-bidding die down I believe that others will see that you are planning a university that is genuinely and valuably new. They will certainly see—and some of them are going to be notably disillusioned by the experience—that the rush to expand in the present decade has brought few distinctive gains. What is most to be feared in the immediate future is the plain inertia of those who will regard themselves (whether justifiably or not) as men who, having met the demands of an era of change, are at last entitled to be left alone. That kind of complacency could be quite fatal to our universities. Against it, the very existence of your committee is at once a safeguard and a continuing challenge.

Yours sincerely,

JAMES DUNDONALD

FLINDERS

A case-study of new university
development in Australia

Peter Karmel
Vice-Chancellor
The Flinders University of South Australia

Since the end of the Second World War there has been a remarkable growth in university education in Australia. In 1946 there were 17,000 students, excluding returned servicemen, in Australian universities; and these constituted 2·3 per cent of the age group 17 to 22 years. By 1956 there were 34,000 students, constituting 4·7 per cent of the age group. By 1965 the figures were 83,000 and 7·5 per cent. Preliminary figures for 1966 put student numbers at over 90,000.

This rapid growth in students has been accompanied by a corresponding growth in the number of universities. At the end of the War there were six universities. The first of these, the University of Sydney, had been established in 1850, and the last, the University of Western Australia, in 1911. Thus there had been no new foundation for thirty-five years. Since 1945 there have been nine new foundations. Of these, the Australian National University (1946), the University of New South Wales (1949), Monash University (1958), Macquarie University (1964), La Trobe University (1964) and the University of Papua and New Guinea (1965) were established as autonomous institutions; whereas the University of New England (1954), the University of Newcastle (1964) and the Flinders University of South Australia (1966) had gained autonomy after an association with an existing institution.

The new universities differ from the old ones in various ways, although many would say that these differences are superficial and that Australian universities are too much of

a single pattern. Some of the new universities have empha-
sized certain activities; for example, research in the Australian National University, technology in the University of
New South Wales, external studies in the University of
New England. Others, such as Macquarie, La Trobe and
Flinders, are attempting different forms of academic organization. When one has been as intimately bound up with the
development of a particular institution as the author has,
one should stick to one's own experience and not pronounce judgement on others. For this reason I am presenting this paper as a case-study in the development of one new
Australian university, which had peculiar origins; and from
this case-study, I shall attempt to draw some quite limited
generalizations about university planning.

(I)

During 1958 the University of Adelaide began to plan the
erection of two major new buildings on its existing 30 acre
site on North Terrace in the city of Adelaide. These new
buildings were necessary to enable the University to cope
with an estimated student enrolment of about 8,000 by 1965.
It soon became apparent that the erection of the new buildings would virtually complete development on North
Terrace, as no further major buildings could be contem-
plated without intolerable overcrowding of the site. This
led to the conclusion that any further expansion of university
activities in South Australia would have to take place on
another site. Such an extension to a second campus was
foreshadowed in 1959 in the University's submission to the
Australian Universities Commission for the 1961–63
triennium. As a result, a small sum (£A6,000) was included
in the University's grant in that triennium for the purpose
of preliminary planning of a new site.

Early in 1961, the South Australian Government indicated its willingness to make available to the University an
area of some 370 acres, known as Bedford Park. Bedford
Park, which had previously been used as a tuberculosis

sanatorium and more recently as a remand home for juvenile delinquents, is situated about seven miles from the centre of Adelaide in the foothills of the Mount Lofty Range. It is a hilly site, rising from 200 feet to 500 feet above sea level. It is intersected by several steep valleys, and contains one gentler valley providing a natural amphitheatre. The site is broad in scale, and exciting and powerful in character. It commands fine views of the sea, city and hills, and has presented a wonderful opportunity for architectural deve-lopment. The site was inspected by the Australian Uni-versities Commission and its use for university purposes was approved. The University Council then appointed a special committee of its own members, including academic mem-bers, to advise it on Bedford Park matters. Towards the middle of 1961 the South Australian Government indicated to the University that it could go ahead with preliminary planning.

At the end of June 1961 I was appointed Principal-designate of Bedford Park and a senior administrative assistant in the University was seconded to act as secretary of all committees concerned with Bedford Park.[1] My appointment was initially a part-time one and I continued with my duties in the Department of Economics. I was instructed to prepare a report on the development of Bedford Park, and the Vice-Chancellor was empowered to appoint such committees as might assist in this task.

Two main advisory committees were appointed to help in the preliminary planning: an academic advisory committee comprising members of the academic staff of the University of Adelaide, and an advisory committee on union, sporting and residential facilities comprising members of the aca-demic staff and others with special interests in these fields. Both committees undertook a considerable amount of work in a short time in preparing their reports.

The first few months after my appointment were occupied with making detailed projections of university student

[1] Mr. H. J. Buchan, later Secretary for Bedford Park, now Registrar of Flinders University.

enrolments for South Australia for the years 1962–75. These formed the basis of the reports on the planning of Bedford Park. By the end of March 1962 the reports on the academic structure and on union, sporting and residential facilities had been adopted by the Council Committee on Bedford Park and were incorporated in a more extensive report to the University Council. This report was adopted by the University Council and formed the basis of a submission to the Australian Universities Commission for the development of Bedford Park for the years 1963–66 inclusive.

In this submission, the Council envisaged that Bedford Park would accept students from the beginning of the academic year in 1966 when the total number of university enrolments (excluding higher degree enrolments) was expected to be 8,650. (In the event the actual numbers turned out to be 8,659—a prime example of the cancellation of errors!) It so happened that the two faculties in which there would be the greatest pressure of numbers at North Terrace were arts and science; and so what was academically desirable coincided with the practical needs of the situation. It was therefore planned that these would be the first faculties to be represented at Bedford Park, although subsequently other faculties would be developed. It was planned that in 1966 Bedford Park should accept 250 arts students, 150 science students and 70 first-year medical students who would complete the remainder of their medical course at North Terrace. Work at Bedford Park would begin in 1966 with first year undergraduate courses and some graduate work. Second, third and fourth year work would be progressively added during 1967, 1968 and 1969. The enrolments planned for Bedford Park (then estimated at about 1,900 arts and science undergraduates by 1970 and nearly 3,000 by 1975) would stablize the arts and science enrolments at North Terrace at about the 1966 levels.

The University Council determined as a matter of policy that Bedford Park should have academic autonomy from the outset. Students would graduate from Bedford Park with degrees of the University of Adelaide, but the professors appointed in charge of disciplines at Bedford Park would be responsible for the design of their own syllabuses, for the structure of the degree courses to be offered, and for the examining. They would in no sense be subject to North Terrace departments; indeed, it was hoped that they would produce syllabuses and courses which differed from those at North Terrace. Bedford Park would appoint senior staff and would have its own academic committees parallel to those at North Terrace. Constitutionally, Bedford Park would be part of the University of Adelaide and would be governed by the University Council in the same way as North Terrace, but its operations would be parallel and not subordinate to North Terrace. The distribution of students between the North Terrace and Bedford Park campuses would be arranged by an admissions procedure, but the details of this procedure were not then determined.

The University of Adelaide's submission on Bedford Park to the Australian Universities Commission was presented at the end of March 1962. The submission incorporated the principles set out above and included estimates of the financial requirements for recurrent and capital expenditure for the year 1963 and the triennium 1964–66. Although Bedford Park would not open until 1966, recurrent grants were requested for earlier years to cover expenditure on planning, administrative staff, library staff, the purchase of library books and the appointment of a limited number of professors. The submission also set out the financial requirements for the erection of the first stages of buildings for the library, the academic schools, the students' union, the administration and some residential accommodation for students; and for site works and services and the establishment of some sporting facilities. The Australian Universities Commission made visits to the University to discuss the Bedford Park proposals and also consulted with the State Government. In October 1962 the University was informed that it might go ahead with its planning for Bedford Park. This was facilitated by special grants for 1963 to finance a limited amount of recurrent expenditure

(£A75,000) and preliminary site works (£A75,000). In its Second Report, the Australian Universities Commission recommended grants of £A143,000, £A267,000 and £A534,000 respectively for the years 1964 to 1966 for recurrent purposes and of £A2,875,000 for capital expenditure during the triennium.

At the end of 1962 I left the Department of Economics to devote my whole time to Bedford Park work; and the University appointed a staff architect for Bedford Park,[1] whose duties were to undertake the site planning of Bedford Park in conjunction with a consultant site planner,[2] and to provide liaison between the University and the buildings architects to be appointed later. Somewhat later the new institution came to be known as 'The University of Adelaide at Bedford Park'.

(II)

In the initial planning on the academic side no firm decisions were made either on academic organization or on the structure of the Bachelor of Arts or Bachelor of Science degrees. However, it was indicated that the academic organization might not be on departmental lines and that the degree structures might be based on principles different from those operating at North Terrace (which are similar to the traditional Australian pattern). It was proposed that Bedford Park might begin with six disciplines in arts and six in science, each with a professor. The foundation disciplines were suggested.

However, at the end of 1962, before advertising for the librarian and the first six professors, the University made an important decision on academic organization. It decided that Bedford Park should be organized in four academic Schools, namely Language and Literature, Social Sciences, Physical Sciences, and Biological Sciences. The School

---

[1] Mr. G. J. Harrison, formerly Staff Architect at North Terrace for the University of Adelaide.

[2] Professor Gordon Stephenson, Consultant Architect, University of Western Australia.

would be the basic academic and administrative unit. In this sense it would replace both faculty and department. In each School there would be a number of professors of whom one would act as Chairman of the School. This system was expected to have certain advantages, including the avoidance of departmentalism; the creation of a unit in which there were always several professors (and hence no 'god-professor'); the encouragement of inter-disciplinary work; and the possibility of covering highly specialized or less usual subjects without creating separate departments for them. Moreover it was intended that the Schools would be physical entities, and that students would pursue courses mainly in one School. This should induce a sense of 'belonging' to a School, which the average pass student taking courses in several different departments has traditionally lacked. Although the University decided on the basic academic structure and on the foundation disciplines before any professors were appointed, the manner in which the Schools would conduct their business, the disciplines which might next be developed, and the nature of the degree courses were left for determination by the professors when they were appointed.

In December 1962 an advertisement was issued for the librarian and for professors of English (School of Language and Literature), History and Economics (School of Social Sciences), Physics and Chemistry (School of Physical Sciences). The main purpose in making these early appointments was to enable the successful candidates to take an active part in the planning of the academic organization and structure of courses and to consult with the architects on the design of the academic buildings. The advertisement for the first professor in the School of Biological Sciences was delayed until March 1963, as the University had been having consultations on the structure and organization of the School.[1] As a result of the consultations, the University

[1] The principal consultant was Dr. (now Sir) Otto Frankel, F.R.S., then of the Commonwealth Scientific and Industrial Research Organization.

decided that the School of Biological Sciences should be a fully integrated one in which there would be no divisions into the traditional disciplines of botany, zoology, etc. The emphasis would rather be on the manner in which the teaching and research was organized, e.g. cellular biology, molecular biology. It was planned that the librarian should take up duty from the middle of 1963; that three of the professors might take up duty at the same time; and that the remaining three professors would take up duty from the beginning of 1964. These positions would, therefore, be filled about two to two and a half years in advance of Bedford Park's taking students.

All preliminary planning for Bedford Park was carried out by committees composed of members of the University at North Terrace. Similarly, membership of Appointment Committees was drawn from the University of Adelaide, although these committees were assisted by assessors from other Australian universities. The planning of Bedford Park has been marked by the ready co-operation and assistance which has been given by members of the North Terrace staff throughout all stages. However, as mentioned above, the policy of the University Council was that, within the general administrative framework already decided, matters of academic policy at Bedford Park should be determined by Bedford Park academic staff. Such policy matters began to be determined by Bedford Park professors from 1964 onwards after the first professors had taken up duty.

In May 1965 the policy of the University Council in ensuring academic separateness for Bedford Park was given formal recognition by a resolution of the University Council that the Principal should be directly responsible to the University Council and its Finance Committee for all the business of Bedford Park. These matters were to be dealt with under one heading on the agenda of the Finance Committee and the Council. The relevant items on the agenda were to be prepared by the Secretary for Bedford Park, who was to have the responsibility, under the Principal, of taking appropriate action resulting from Finance Committee and Council decisions.

In January 1963 the Bedford Park Planning Office was set up in rented premises in the city where it was possible to bring together under the one roof the staff engaged in the Bedford Park planning. The Bedford Park Planning Office continued in these premises until permanent accommodation became available on the site late in 1965. However, most of the professors were accommodated within their corresponding departments at North Terrace, where they were provided with appropriate facilities and the opportunity to engage in such teaching or research as they wished.

Throughout the early months of 1963, the site planners worked out the basic concepts of the site development plan. Early in 1963 a firm of architects was appointed to design the first stages of the academic, library, union and administrative buildings.[1] At the same time engineering and structural consultants[2] for site works and services and buildings and a landscaping consultant[3] were appointed.

In planning for Bedford Park, it had been envisaged that residential accommodation for students would be provided on the site for a substantially higher proportion of students than that provided by the independent colleges affiliated with North Terrace. The planning of residential accommodation has been developed along the lines of a university hall of residence comprising a complex of buildings housing up to, perhaps, 800 students in four or five separate courts, each with its separate dining hall but sharing common kitchen and catering facilities. The first stage of this complex, which was originally planned to be completed by 1966, was to include the central kitchen and residential and dining accommodation for 200 students. Early in 1963, the Staff

[1] Hassell, McConnell and Partners.
[2] Professor F. B. Bull, Professor of Civil Engineering, University of Adelaide, and Kinnaird, Hill and Associates.
[3] Professor L. D. Pryor, Professor of Botany, Australian National University.

Architect was appointed as design architect for the first stage of the residential accommodation.

By the middle of 1963 the site plan was virtually complete. It was based on the assumption that Bedford Park would ultimately cater for about 6,000 students, a number which will probably be achieved early in the 1980s. In May 1963 the University Council gave approval to the basic site plan design. This included the siting and massing of the first academic buildings. In the meantime, briefs had been prepared of the requirements for the first stages of the academic, library, union and administration buildings and the multi-purpose theatre; and planning of these buildings by the architects was commenced in May, 1963.

The architects' planning proceeded in close liaison with the site planners, the engineering and structural consultant, the Secretary and myself. Regular weekly meetings were held to discuss the design and function of buildings and to ensure that they met the requirements of the University. Advice on design of academic buildings was sought from members of the North Terrace staff when appropriate members of the Bedford Park staff were not available. Preliminary sketch plans for site works and services and for buildings (other than students' residences) were completed during the second half of 1963. Final sketch plans for buildings were approved by the Australian Universities Commission before the end of that year. Detailed working drawings then followed; and the two major building contracts were let in October and December 1964. The buildings were completed progressively over the period October 1965 to February 1966. These buildings will cope with an enrolment of rather less than 1,000 students, but the design of the second stage of some of the buildings is proceeding during 1966. The hall of residence has been delayed because State Government approval for the necessary expenditure has not yet been given.

Construction work for site works and services began in October 1963 and continued throughout 1964. Roads were constructed; water, gas, electricity and telephone services were installed; and playing fields were prepared. The Curator of Grounds took up duty in July 1963. By the middle of 1966 he had already completed an extensive tree planting programme of some 6,000 trees, established a nursery containing more than 1,000 trees and shrubs and developed 25 acres of playing fields (which were opened by Sir Donald Bradman on 9 March 1966); he had in addition, landscaped a twelve acre park and lake at the heart of the academic area, and three courtyards among the buildings. Sports changing rooms were constructed in 1964.

Early in 1963 the librarian was appointed; and he took up duty in June 1963. He immediately began the purchase of books and periodicals for the library and the appointment of staff to handle their processing. By the end of 1964 he had a staff of seventeen and had accessioned nearly 40,000 volumes. The library opened in 1966 with some 60,000 volumes on the shelves, catalogued and classified, with current subscriptions to some 1,800 serials and with a staff of twenty-nine members.

During 1963 the first six professors were appointed; and a further eight were appointed in the next year. These have been available for consultations concerning buildings and academic courses. Most of them were in Adelaide by October 1965. The Chairmen of the four Schools were appointed in 1964.[1] The initial fourteen chairs were as follows: English, French, Spanish, History, Economics, Geography, Political Theory and Institutions, Physics, Chemistry (two chairs in the fields of organic chemistry and physical chemistry), Mathematics (in the field of pure mathematics), Biology (three chairs in the fields of genetics, biochemistry and biophysics). Ten additional chairs have already been created, which have been filled or are in the process of being filled. These are Drama, Philosophy, Social Administration, Education, Social Psychology,

[1] Language and Literature: R. W. V. Elliott, Professor of English; Social Sciences: O. O. G. M. MacDonagh, Professor of History; Physical Sciences: M. H. Brennan, Professor of Physics; Biological Sciences: A. M. Clark, Professor of Biology.

Mathematics (three chairs in the fields of pure mathematics, applied mathematics and mathematical statistics), Physics (in the field of theoretical physics) and Biology (in the field of microbial genetics).

During 1964 the University Council decided to discontinue the subgraduate diploma in social studies which had been offered at North Terrace, to transfer the staff of the Department of Social Studies to the School of Social Sciences at Bedford Park, to initiate a postgraduate diploma in the field of social work at Bedford Park, and to create a chair in Social Administration to supervise the postgraduate diploma and other relevant work in the School of Social Sciences.

Also during 1964 there arose the question of the relation between the University and the Teachers College which was to be built on twenty acres of the Bedford Park site which had been earmarked by the Government for that purpose. By decision of the State Department of Education, most of the students at the Teachers College will be university students. In order to foster a close relationship between the work of the College and the University, the University Council and the State Department of Education decided to make provision for a joint appointment of Principal of the Bedford Park Teachers College and Professor of Education in the School of Social Sciences. The Department agreed to give the Principal the same freedom to experiment in the work of the College as the University at Bedford Park itself had. Legislation to enable this arrangement was passed by the South Australian Parliament in 1965; and the Professor-Principal was appointed in 1966.

During the first four months of 1965 about forty-five non-professorial academic posts were advertised, including senior lectureships in Music and in Fine Arts in the School of Language and Literature. By the middle of the year most of these were filled. Some of these members of staff arrived in Adelaide in the last three months of the year, and the rest during the first three months of 1966. A small number of senior administrative and technical staff were appointed

early in 1965, but the main recruitment of technical and
administrative staff took place towards the end of the year.
By the middle of 1966, there were two hundred and eleven
full-time staff of all kinds on the payroll. Recruitment for
additional non-professorial staff for 1967 was well under
way by the middle of 1966.

In September 1965 the University appointed a Director
of Union Services to supervise the operation of the Union
and the Sports Association and to assist students in initiat-
ing extra-curricular activities. A small Union Advisory
Committee was formed, to which two students, appointed
by the Students Association Committee, were added early
in the first term of 1966. By the middle of that term a
number of student societies was in vigorous operation and
the University was represented by teams in seven sporting
competitions. The Union Advisory Committee and the
Students' Association Committee, as interim bodies, prepared constitutions for their permanent successors, the
Union Board, the Sports Association Council and the
Students' Representative Council. These were approved by
the University Council and came into operation in September 1966. The Board governing the Union comprises
representatives from the University Council, the academic
staff and the students. Students make up about half the
membership of the Union Board.

The University is operating a health service with the help
of medical practitioners working on a sessional basis. The
University also appointed a student counsellor in the middle
of 1966.

(III)

It might be thought that the close relationship between
Bedford Park and North Terrace would have resulted in the
appointment of staff, of which a high proportion were
members of staff of North Terrace, or at least were graduates
of the University of Adelaide. It is true that the Secretary,
the Staff Architect and myself (the three people concerned

141

with planning from the outset) had been members of the staff at North Terrace; but for the rest there was relatively little recruitment from Adelaide. Of the twenty-one professors appointed by the middle of 1966, six had been members of the staff at North Terrace and only one was an Adelaide graduate. Of the sixty-seven non-professorial members of the academic staff, six had been members of the staff at North Terrace, and fourteen were Adelaide graduates.

Bedford Park was created, and its early development took place, while Sir Thomas Playford was Premier of the State. The policy of his Government was that Bedford Park should remain a part of the University of Adelaide; and that, even though it had a separate budget, it should be governed by the Council of the University of Adelaide. The reasons for this policy appeared to be that by these means it was hoped to avoid undesirable competition for staff and funds; to maintain good relations between the two institutions; and to facilitate dealings between the two institutions and the Government.

In March 1965 the Playford Government's record twenty-six years of office was terminated by its defeat by the Labour Party. The Labour Party had included in its election programme the translation of Bedford Park into a separate and independent university. Towards the end of 1965 the new Government prepared a Bill to create Bedford Park an independent university with the name 'The Flinders University of South Australia', after the great explorer and hydrographer, Matthew Flinders, who had circumnavigated Australia in the years 1801 to 1803, and had sailed, in 1802, in waters overlooked by the Bedford Park site. The Bill was finally passed by both Houses of Parliament and was assented to on 17 March 1966.

The Flinders University of South Australia Act, which came into force on 1 July 1966—exactly five years after my appointment as Principal-designate—is modelled (except for the composition of the Council) on the University of Adelaide Act. The Act places the whole management of the

University in the hands of a Council with powers to make Statutes and Regulations subject to the approval of the Governor-in-Council.[1] The Council comprises twenty-seven members: the Chancellor, the Vice-Chancellor, the Director of Education, five members of Parliament elected by Parliament, a nominee each of the Chambers of Manufactures and Commerce jointly, the Trades and Labour Council and the Government, two professors and two non-professorial members of the academic staff elected by the academic staff, the President of the Students' Representative Council, eight members elected by Convocation (initially these will be elected by the corresponding body of the University of Adelaide, with the restriction that four of them shall be members of the academic staff of Flinders), and up to three members co-opted by the Council. The Council held its first meeting on 11 July 1966, and elected as Chancellor, Emeritus Professor Sir Mark Mitchell (formerly Professor of Biochemistry and Deputy Vice-Chancellor of the University of Adelaide, and son of Sir William Mitchell, a former Professor, Vice-Chancellor and Chancellor of the University of Adelaide).

Towards the end of 1964 the organization of the Schools had been formalized by the passing of a statute by the University Council. This statute defined the duties of the Schools and the manner in which they would conduct their business. The general policy of each School is determined by a Board comprising all the academic members of the School. The day-to-day business, however, is conducted by Standing Committees each of which comprises the professors and an equal number of non-professorial staff elected by the Board of each School. The first chairmen were appointed by the Council. In future chairmen, who need not be professors, will be appointed on four-year terms on the recommendations of the Standing Committees. A chairman may act for a second four-year term; but in order

[1] After 1971, they will also be subject to the approval of Convocation, which will comprise the graduates of the University and such other members as the Council may determine.

to extend a term beyond eight years it will be necessary for the Standing Committee to make a special recommendation to the University Council.

The committee structure evolved during the latter part of 1965. After full discussion by the Boards of the Schools and by an interim acedemic committee representative of the Schools, the structure was formally adopted by the Council in July 1966. There is no Professorial Board in the traditional sense. Instead, there is an Academic Committee comprising the Chairmen, the Vice-Chairmen and a third representative of each School (of these, at least one must be non-professorial), the Chairman of the Research Committee, the librarian and one member of the Council. The Vice-Chancellor is Chairman. The Academic Committee advises the Council on all academic matters, and is the channel through which all proposals and recommendations from the Boards of the Schools pass to the Council for approval.

The other two key committees are the Finance and Buildings Committee and the Allocations Committee. The former comprises Council members, including at least two academic members of Council, and elects its own Chairman. It advises the Council on the financial operations of the University, on terms and conditions of appointment of staff, and on the university site and buildings. The function of the Allocations Committee is to fit the requests of the Schools, Library and Administration for development into the available budgetary resources. It comprises the Vice-Chancellor as Chairman, the Chairmen of the Schools and the Chairman of the Finance and Buildings Committee. It must have regard to the policy of the Academic Committee and reports to the Council through the Academic Committee, which may forward comments on the report to the Council.

In addition to these two committees, the usual battery of Research Committee, Library Committee, Technical Staff Committee, Study Leave Committee, Matriculation Board, and so on, will operate. These committees are relatively small (usually about eight members) but their constitutions have been designed to make it possible for those members of the academic staff who are competent and willing to take part in committee work to do so irrespective of status.

Every member of the academic staff is a member of the Board of his School; and it is at this level, which impinges directly on his academic work, that he can exert an influence on academic policy. Apart from this, the restricted size of the committees means that there may be many members of staff, including some of the most senior ones, who have little contact with colleagues in other Schools or with general university policy. For this reason it is intended to circulate the agenda and minutes of the Academic Committee and of the Council itself to all members of the academic staff. In addition the Vice-Chancellor will hold an annual meeting of academic and other senior staff at which he will report past progress and future plans, and where general discussion will take place.

Procedures for making appointments were also approved by the University Council in July 1966. These follow those which Bedford Park had adopted from the University of Adelaide. Professors are appointed by the Council on the recommendation of *ad hoc* Appointment Committees, chaired by the Vice-Chancellor and appointed by the Council on his recommendation. Non-professorial academic staff appointments are approved by the Vice-Chancellor on the recommendation of the appropriate School Standing Appointments Committee.

(IV)

Preliminary discussions on the structures of the Bachelor of Arts and Bachelor of Science degrees began as soon as the first professors were available. The general nature of the structures was developed in 1964, and was approved, in principle, by the University Council about the middle of that year. Documents outlining the structures of the two degrees were submitted·to meetings of the relevant Heads of Departments in the Faculties of Arts and Science at North

Terrace for discussion and comment but were not subject to their approval. The details of the degrees were developed further during 1965 and were approved by the University Council before the end of that year.

The degree courses differ materially from those at North Terrace. They are built upon the principle of offering the students a choice of a limited number of 'programmes', rather than allowing students to aggregate credits at choice within a framework of rules. Although students usually pursue their studies in more than one School, the programmes are being designed so that a student will be associated mainly with one School. These arrangements have the objectives on the one hand of building up an integrated course of study, and on the other hand of producing in the student a sense of 'belonging' to a particular School. In Arts, the programmes are based on a study in depth of two disciplines (about two-thirds of the work) together with three cognate courses bearing some relation to the major disciplines. In Science, all students read a common first year (Physics, Chemistry, Biology and Mathematics) and then specialize in a single or double disciplinary programme. In both Arts and Science it is intended to examine by years rather than by courses, except that special arrangements are being made for part-time students.

The 1966 academic year began on 7 March, when 178 first-year undergraduates in Arts, 133 in Science, 70 in Medicine (to transfer to the University of Adelaide at the end of their first year) and 35 graduate students were enrolled. The buildings had just been completed and the academic staff gathered. The Library was in working order, although with few days to spare; the Union was operating, although the menu of the refectory was scarcely *cordon bleu*. On 25 March Her Majesty Queen Elizabeth the Queen Mother officially opened the University.

A new university faces many problems, but perhaps the fundamental one is that it is presented with a mass of raw students, most of whom have never been near a university, many of whom may be resentful at being there rather than at a long-established university, and practically all of whom are lost in a strange place. It is perhaps a measure of the success of the opening of Flinders that within two weeks the student body was sufficiently cohesive to form a mass protest at the invitation of only a few of their number to the official opening ceremony of 'their' university, that before the end of the first term the students were aggressively pro Flinders; and that on 1 July, when the Act was proclaimed, 'Independence Day' was celebrated by them by a six-course breakfast with champagne at 7.15 in the morning followed by a march to the statue of Matthew Flinders in the city, where independence was proclaimed! I attribute this measure of success largely to the completion on time of the first stage of the buildings which embraced a 'whole university' with permanent library and union, and to the compactness of the siting of the buildings so that the movement of staff and students through the courts and the mall produced a sense of life and busyness right from the start. The presence of the students on these first days was the catalyst which brought the University to life.

The division of Arts and Science students between North Terrace and Bedford Park was effected in 1966 by a centralized admissions procedure. It was agreed that students should be offered places at either North Terrace or Bedford Park as far as possible in conformity with their wishes, but in a manner which would produce roughly similar distributions of talent at both campuses. This procedure worked satisfactorily. Many students opted for Bedford Park, but nevertheless there were many others who were offered places there, although they would have preferred to attend North Terrace. Bedford Park benefited from this arrangement, for it prevented a creaming-off of talent by North Terrace and it maintained the academic quality of the student body.

Since the independence of Flinders, any such arrangement must be by agreement between universities, rather than by decision within a university. Flinders University and the University of Adelaide have agreed to operate a centralized admissions procedure, at least for the 1967–69 triennium. In addition, Flinders has agreed to take certain numbers of first year students in Medicine, Dentistry and Agricultural Science who will take a normal science first year at Flinders and then transfer to Adelaide; the object of this is to assist the Faculty of Science at Adelaide by reducing the burden of the so-called service courses provided for the professional faculties. The method of division of students will be by student preference; if the number preferring one institution exceeds that institution's quota, a selection based on academic merit will be made.

(V)

I have outlined in some detail the various stages in the foundation of Bedford Park as a case-study in the development of a new university institution. Some general observations arising from the Bedford Park experience may now be pertinent.

It is important to emphasize the limited generality of the conclusions which can be drawn from what has happened at Bedford Park. Within the Australian setting, the Bedford Park development has been unique. The other new universities founded in Australia since the end of the Second World War have started either as university colleges of an older university or as new foundations governed initially by interim councils. In the former cases, the colleges started by being academically subservient to the parent institution with little or no control over syllabuses and examining, let alone over the structure of degrees. They then faced some years of struggle to win an increasing degree of autonomy and finally complete autonomy. In the latter cases, the interim councils were obliged to make important decisions of policy before the existence of vice-chancellors or professors to advise them.

Bedford Park was not a college of the University of Adelaide, for it was academically autonomous from the start; rather it was the University of Adelaide *at* Bedford Park. Moreover, it has never had an interim council of the kind usual for new foundations. Bedford Park has been unique for three other reasons. First, it had a relatively ample planning period. Detailed budgets and programmes had been worked out before any substantial funds were forthcoming. Thus although the building schedule was tight (over £A2¼ million worth of buildings were constructed in fifteen months) preliminary planning was detailed and thorough. Secondly, I was in the privileged position of playing a key role in the planning from almost the moment of conception; I did not face existing commitments or an existing time-table, other than the requirement to take students in 1966 almost five years ahead of my appointment. Thirdly, Bedford Park received its independence, perhaps unexpectedly early, virtually from the moment it admitted students.

The Bedford Park approach derived from two conditions. The first was political: the State Government did not wish a second separate university to be established. The second was the determination on the part of the parent university that Bedford Park should be run as nearly as possible as a separate institution. Combined, these two considerations produced an arrangement, the nearest analogy to which is that of a holding company (the University Council) and two operating companies (the North Terrace and the Bedford Park campuses).

Given the approach, its successful implementation was made possible by four factors. First, as has been pointed out, the University Council was resolved that Bedford Park should be genuinely academically autonomous from the outset. Secondly, the Australian Universities Commission made recommendations relating to grants for Bedford Park which were separate from those for the rest of the University of Adelaide. Academic autonomy presented the possibility of developing courses and syllabuses not only independent of, but quite distinct from, those at North Terrace; financial autonomy removed from within the University competition for funds. Thus the areas in which conflict might occur between parent and offspring were reduced in the foundation stages. Thirdly, there was a close personal relationship between myself and the Vice-Chancellor of the University of Adelaide (Sir Henry Basten) who was determined that Bedford Park should have the freedom to develop in its own ways. Finally, there was also a relationship of confidence and understanding between myself and the University Council, of which I have been an elected member since 1955.

The manner in which Bedford Park has been developed has had considerable advantages. In seeking academic staff we have gained from the prestige which attaches to the University of Adelaide. Of course, we should not have so benefited had it not been made quite clear that we were academically independent of North Terrace. We have had available advice and help, which has been freely sought and generously given. We have had colleagues at North Terrace who have been genuinely and unselfishly interested in the Bedford Park development, which has been seen as a means both of assisting North Terrace to contain its numbers and strengthening the academic community in Adelaide. When professors were appointed two or three years in advance of buildings for them, accommodation and facilities for research and teaching have been made available for them in the appropriate North Terrace departments. The library was accommodated for over two years, at some inconvenience to its landlord, in one part of the Barr Smith Library at North Terrace, which also provided assistance in a number of other directions.

Moreover, the government of Bedford Park in its early days by an existing and experienced University Council has proved of great value. We had available to us sets of procedures in making appointments, in determining conditions of appointments and in other matters, which, although perhaps not ideal for us in the long run, nevertheless provided us with working practice. We did not in the initial stages have to set up a separate accounting section. Our book-keeping was done for us at North Terrace, although we did, of course, fully control our own budgeting.

These have all been advantages to Bedford Park. The operation of North Terrace and Bedford Park as one university rather than as two separate ones also facilitated the establishment of a rational admissions procedure. New students wishing to embark on courses available at both campuses applied for admission and were offered a place at one or other of the campuses. This resulted in less delay and frustration for students as well as for the two universities. We have also been able to achieve some specialization in the disciplines which are being offered at North Terrace and Bedford Park. For example, Spanish and Social Administration are available at Bedford Park and not at North Terrace; on the other hand it is not planned to develop classical studies at Bedford Park, which are well developed at North Terrace. Moreover, we intend not to embark on unnecessary duplication of faculties.

Finally, there is another advantage which has been of some value to Bedford Park but has probably accrued mainly to North Terrace: we have avoided competing for staff in terms of salaries and conditions of employment. These have been uniform between the two campuses; and we have operated a gentleman's agreement in relation to the transfer of staff from North Terrace to Bedford Park. North Terrace staff have, naturally, been quite free to apply for any advertised Bedford Park posts. In making appointments of these staff to Bedford Park posts, however, one convention has been strictly observed; namely, when we have appointed a North Terrace member of staff to the same grade at Bedford Park, we have done so without increase of salary. This has avoided the luring of staff from North Terrace to Bedford Park by payment of extra salary increments. Staff may still be induced to move to Bedford Park through choice or promotion, but such appointments are made on a recommendation from the Appointments Committee that the candidate is worthy of the higher post; and, until the independence of Flinders, there was a small element of North Terrace representation on Appointments Committees. So far we have carefully followed this convention.

Some people have transferred to Bedford Park with and without promotion, but we have run into no difficulties.

The advantages which stemmed from the arrangements operating up to independence were very considerable. However, there were disadvantages also. These arose mainly because the parent institution had an interest in the consequences of the activities of the new institution on itself. Thus, despite the strong support at North Terrace for innovation at Bedford Park, some demands developed for Bedford Park to offer a similar range of courses and services, so that the new institution could relieve the older one of students in most courses. Consequently some pressure on the plans of the new institution was inevitable; and seemed likely to increase as time went by. Indeed, it could be argued that the main benefits of the arrangement as far as Bedford Park was concerned had already been reaped by the end of 1965, and that independence came at an ideal time. Lack of freedom in respect of terms and conditions of employment may be thought to be a handicap; but, in my view, both institutions would be likely to suffer from competitive bargaining for staff. On the other hand, the association of the two institutions within the one university made it difficult for the new institution to acquire independent identity and status; for example, it was not represented on the Australian Vice-Chancellors' Committee and was not recognized as a separate institution for a number of other purposes.

Accordingly, however smoothly the arrangements worked over the planning period from 1961 to 1965, difficulties and risks of disagreement seemed likely to occur when Bedford Park started to operate as a teaching institution. These were heightened when occupation of the Bedford Park site produced seven miles of physical separation and made attendance at meetings difficult. Moreover, the practices and precedents of a large and slowly growing university, as Adelaide will now be, do not necessarily suit the needs of a small and rapidly growing one. The need to conform to these practices and precedents seemed likely to become increasingly onerous; and it was difficult for the smaller institution to exercise much influence on them, although its absolute rate of recruitment was actually much greater than that of the larger institution. These difficulties and dangers were appreciated by both parties; and when the new Government asked the Council of the University of Adelaide for its views on the granting of independence to Bedford Park, the Council unanimously resolved to inform the Government that it supported independence and that independence should take place forthwith. There was a general feeling that relations between Bedford Park and North Terrace had been and were at that time so harmonious that the break should come before they deteriorated. This was in the belief that collaboration and co-operation would be more likely between independent institutions. There is already evidence of the validity of this. Indeed the Council of the University showed great wisdom both in creating Bedford Park initially autonomous, and in so readily agreeing to the separation of the offspring which it had so tenderly and unselfishly nurtured. It was fitting that at the Royal opening of Flinders (which preceded the proclamation of the Act by some months) the Chancellor of the University of Adelaide (Sir George Ligertwood) should preside and that the Council of the University of Adelaide should still be the governing body of the new university.

On the purely administrative (or managerial) side, the establishment of Bedford Park did not produce any serious problems. The programme of physical facilities (site works and services, sports fields, buildings), the establishment of the library, and the recruitment of staff all ran within a few weeks of the timetable laid down at the commencement of operations. Here it was largely a matter of obtaining the services of a limited number of able people, and trusting them within a routine of frequent consultation.

We also derived great help from the very detailed plans which had been made in the preparation of the original submission to the Australian Universities Commission. We had specified precisely numbers and type of staff, the

L   153 dates on which they would take up duty, detailed items of recurrent expenditure, and an elaborate outline of our capital needs. When the Australian Universities Commission did not provide grants to meet fully our submission, the original schedules were immediately revised; and we have used them as a continuing frame of reference in conjunction with flexible budgeting procedures.

The making of *academic* plans is, however, quite another question. To what extent can plans be formulated in the early days of the foundation of an institution about the academic organization, the range of disciplines to be taught, and the structure of degrees? Clearly it is not difficult to make plans, but can they be made to stick?

In planning at this level one is torn between two objectives. On the one hand, there is the desire to innovate; on the other, to delay decisions until academics are available to give advice. These objectives are likely to conflict because of the innate conservatism of most academics—a conservatism, incidentally, which does not appear to be correlated with age. Members of the academic staff tend to be greatly influenced by their own academic experiences. This is a strong force for conservatism. Moreover, professors are not likely to accept readily academic plans in advance of their appointment. Even where a group of professors sympathetic to a particular line of development is gathered, the filling of additional chairs is likely to produce competing views. One expects a first-class scholar to have strong views about his and allied subjects. Consensus among the first-rate is almost a contradiction in terms.

At Bedford Park a limited number of foundation disciplines were necessarily decided in advance of any academic appointments; but the nature of the second batch of chairs underwent minor modification as a result of the first academic appointments. The academic organization of the four Schools was laid down in advance. However, the statute governing the Schools and the conduct of their business was drafted in consultation with the first six professors and was modified in accordance with their advice. The system of committee organization was not finalized until the academic staff for the first year (1966) was virtually complete.

The School system is designed to avoid the rigidities of the customary departmental one. In principle the School is meant to be large enough to contain at least five or six professors (and thus to avoid the dangers of the monolithic department) and small enough to avoid such a large academic staff as to frustrate its having any real influence on academic policy. The School is thus a more 'open' organization than the department, and is deliberately flexible in its conception. With the School system we shall have at least the opportunity of evolving into something different from the standard pattern. If we revert to type—and there is always this risk—at least we shall have given a new kind of organization a chance.

(VI)

The degree structure was designed by the first few professors and approved by the University Council in principle. Subsequent professors have been presented with the general principles of the structure and have been asked to work within the general pattern. Apart from minor modifications, this pattern has so far been followed.

The conflict between the desire to innovate and to plan strictly on the basis of academic advice is a very real one. Given fifteen or twenty professors and no commitments with respect to academic organization or degree structure, a pattern not unlike that existing in established Australian universities is likely to emerge—largely as a highest common factor of agreement. Consequently, innovation requires certain things to be laid down in advance. However, in my view, these should merely set the stage and establish a framework within which there may be a natural evolution of organization and structure. This should be so, partly because the academic staff *is* essentially the university and partly because individual members of the academic staff are more expert within their own fields than any administrator.

If we have had a philosophy at Bedford Park, this has been it. We have had plenty of ideas as to how we should like to see Bedford Park develop, but no central theme or themes have been laid down. We have not tried to impose detailed theories of how Bedford Park should be organized or its courses developed; rather have we attempted to provide a setting in which new approaches to academic organization and to the structure of courses may eventually emerge.

By and large we have so far stuck to our original plans. However, some strains emerged quite early in the piece. There are one or two professors who feel uneasy in the School system and would undoubtedly prefer the more straightforward departmental structure; and there are some members of the academic staff who would prefer shorter terms of office for the Chairmen of the Schools, and thus a more automatic rotation of this post than was originally intended. Similarly there are some who believe in giving students the greatest freedom of choice in their selection of courses; and this conflicts with the principles of our degree structures. Just how much of our original academic planning will remain intact at the end of a decade, or even at the end of five years, is a nice question. But, provided we produce a dynamic lively institution, it may not matter a great deal.

Since the members of the academic staff are responsible for ensuring that the university fulfils its functions, their views should carry great weight; and they are, of course, likely to attempt to modify the shape of the institution in accordance with those views. The way in which a university ultimately handles its affairs may well turn out to be different from the way in which it was planned or from any rules laid down by statute. This was recognized early in the planning of Bedford Park; and we have attempted to innovate more by producing a flexible organization which does not reflect past practices than by laying down any rigid specifications.

A SOCIETY AND ITS UNIVERSITIES
The case of New Zealand

W. H. Oliver
Professor of History
Massey University, Palmerston North
New Zealand

Since the Second World War the New Zealand universities have been trying to cope simultaneously with two major pressures: a mounting social demand for higher education, and a persistent academic demand for higher standards. These demands are not readily reconciled. Even in the best-financed of circumstances the argument that more equals worse is not to be overthrown without effort, and the New Zealand universities are not well-financed. This is the major, but it is not the only, perplexity confronting the New Zealand university teacher. An ideological imperative has cut across the social-academic tension in the same twenty-year period, a conviction that the country should explore the implications of its South Pacific location, that it should so find its way to national maturity, and that the universities should lead this intellectual revolution. At eccentric extremes, such opinion is clothed in a vague and patently misleading vocabulary by which New Zealanders are characterized as either Asians or 'white Polynesians'. More soberly, it requires that Japan, China and India be set alongside, if not in the place of, Greece, Rome and Western Europe. Sometimes this ideological pressure reinforces social pressures; for instance, when the universities are asked to give businessmen and civil servants a smattering of conversational Japanese or Malay, or to produce schoolteachers who know 'something about Asia'. But equally it can reinforce the internal academic pressure, as universities grope towards specialized programmes in

Asian languages, history and sociology, Pacific archaeology and anthropology. Here, though, the perpetual shortage of cash exerts its pressures: it is cheaper to hand out a smattering of Malay than employ a sinologist, and so it is more likely to happen.

The New Zealand universities are shaped by the interaction of these four pressures: financial stringency, social demand, academic demand, ideological reorientation. The last, indeed, is still considerably an 'ought' rather than an 'is'. That it should be so, a quarter-century after the fall of Singapore, indicates, as well as mere conservatism, the constantly crippling results of being hard up, and the energy expended in the mere effort to maintain and improve standards.

These four factors, their nature and their interplay, determine the character of university education in New Zealand. Defining them leads us to ask, not simply 'What kind of universities are there in New Zealand?' but also, and first, 'What kind of society is New Zealand?'

I *Social Demand*

When, in the period running from the 1870s to the early twentieth century, university colleges were set up in Dunedin, Christchurch, Auckland and Wellington, as part of an institution which must have strong claims to be regarded as the world's most calamitous example of a federal university, it was made clear by the promoters that they were trying to meet two social demands—for culture, and for professional training. Because, in this same period, New Zealand completed her evolution towards political democracy, and established a pattern of steady upward social mobility (with a low ceiling); because, further, the country was hard up for most of this period; and because, finally, a marked intolerance of eccentricity and certain kinds of excellence established itself as a leading characteristic of New Zealand society, it was probable that this twin demand would be answered in an egalitarian, inexpensive and conformist manner. As a result, it is very doubtful if it is at all proper to talk about university education as a regular occurrence in New Zealand till well into the twentieth century: until, perhaps, after the Second World War.

To disseminate culture, poorly-paid professors heading minute departments taught an immense range of subjects, produced little research, and were not readily distinguishable from school teachers. The level was low, alarmingly and shamefully so, to those university teachers who headed a movement for reform in the 1920s, men who had come to realize that they lived in one of the world's academic slums. Still, the social demand was being met; languages, literature, history and philosophy, of a kind, and a number of useful skills, were being taught to many young New Zealanders. In the educational system as a whole, two significant barriers to upward progress existed: between the primary and secondary schools, and between the latter and the university colleges. In theory, the second barrier was the less formidable. All who, at secondary school, passed a University Entrance examination *could* enter for a far from exacting degree course, as full-time students, as part-time students or as exempted students (i.e. not attending lectures, but reading textbooks and sitting examinations), though only a smallish proportion did so. The system was one of theoretical egalitarianism restricted by examinations. Actually social and economic restrictions operated; neither money nor motivation was especially common in the lower social strata. When, in the course of the 1930s and 1940s, the barrier between primary and secondary schools was removed, and the entrance examination was (for most entrants) replaced by a system of accrediting by the schools, and when, too, affluence made secondary education normal and tertiary education more usual, then the egalitarian pattern lost all its institutional and many of its social limitations. But, as will be shown later, some real social restrictions have persisted.

The expansion of the mid-twentieth century is illustrated in the following table:

EXPANSION OF SCHOOL AND UNIVERSITY
POPULATIONS
(1924 = 100)

	Primary	Secondary	University	Population
1924	100	100	100	100
1929	103	129	110	109
1934	96	137	118	116
1939	96	163	137	121
1944	101	181	180	123
1949	118	215	285	139
1954	152	323	268	154
1959	169	463	324	172

Over the 1920s and the 1930s the universities expanded
rather more rapidly than the population, but not, in these
decades of uncertainty, depression and recovery, in any
spectacular manner. But the secondary school population,
over the same period, expanded very considerably, more
slowly in the acutely depressed early 1930s, but rapidly in
the more buoyant late 30s, a period, further, in which the
examination bar between primary and secondary schooling
was removed. The university enrolment boomed over the
war, and especially the post-war, period, a major increase
reflecting both the pent-up demand of ex-servicemen and
the constantly expanding secondary school rolls. In this
period (the middle 1940s) accrediting replaced examination
as the normal method of qualifying for university entrance,
the school-leaving age was raised, and post-war affluence
enabled young people to stay longer in the educational
process. The very rapid increase of the secondary rolls over
the 1950s (and into the 1960s) led to an increasing demand
for places at the universities. The expansion shown here
has not significantly altered the nature of the universities,
but rather has magnified the scale of the pattern already
established. Professional training was a major university
concern from the outset: medicine, engineering, dentistry,
mining, agriculture, forestry, law, accountancy, 'home

science', architecture, journalism, were all established by or during the 1920s. The colleges vied with each other for the privilege of maintaining 'special' schools, so that though certain specializations were maintained (e.g. medicine at Otago, and engineering at Canterbury) there was also considerable duplication and waste leading to inefficiency and an avoidable depression of standards. Thus social demand created a permanent pattern: any professional group seeking training for its entrants and status for its practitioners looks confidently to the universities to undertake the work, not to other forms of tertiary education, which in fact play a less significant role than they might in the country's educational system.[1] J. C. Beaglehole, the historian of the University of New Zealand, remarked upon 'the odd New Zealand persuasion that every useful art, to be really useful, must be elevated to the status of a university matter, with examination and diploma'. (*The University of New Zealand*, O.U.P., 1937, p. 257). Currently, the New Zealand universities provide special training for, among others, town planners and valuers, criminologists and welfare workers, physical education specialists and clinical psychologists, surveyors and horticulturalists, wildlife managers and wool-classers. By no means all of these courses are reserved for graduates; on the contrary, an unhappily long list could be made of courses leading to a university qualification which do not require of their students even the usual entrance qualification. In such ways as these the demand for specialized training, normally based upon a very slight general education, has given the New Zealand universities a disproportionately heavy technological and vocational commitment. Further, so closely are the arts faculties related to the teaching profession, and the science faculties to government and other scientific institu-

---

[1] Teacher training, curiously enough, has never been a direct university concern, though it is fully as suited to a university context as many actual university activities. Tentative steps are being taken to integrate the work of universities and teacher training colleges.

tions as well as to the schools, that the New Zealand universities as a whole have an overwhelmingly vocational function. The clergy has been the only professional group regarded with persistent suspicion, so vital has secularism been as an educational principle. Even so, formally at Otago, and informally at Auckland and Canterbury, some provision has recently been made for its needs.

In general, up to the Second World War, the nature of social demand helped produce university institutions of a distinctly unambitious kind, discharging the function of community colleges and trade-training centres. It was not that excellence did not, from time to time occur; it was rather the case that it could not be counted on, nor could it be either consolidated or retained. Lord Rutherford, Sir Ronald Syme, Sir Raymond Firth, came *from* and went *through* the New Zealand university system in the way that other expatriates, such as Katherine Mansfield and Frances Hodgskins, came from and went through not dissimilar segments of New Zealand society. The university colleges did not show any marked capacity to retain local excellence (or draw it back after a spell overseas) or to attract overseas talent till the 1930s, and then only marginally. Nor is such capacity notable in the 1960s.

Judged simply from the standpoint of the demand placed upon it by society, the New Zealand university system has performed satisfactorily, and continues to do so. But more recently severe tensions have been generated as internal academic pressure has attempted to drive up standards. Politicians, administrators (some within, some without the universities) and other guardians of society, such as editorialists and editorial correspondents, ring alarm bells when they observe the statistical gap between university entrants and university graduates. They are readier to identify waste and incompetence within the system than lack of ability among entrants; to see the standard of graduation as too high rather than the standard of entry as too low. These alarm bells will ring the more frequently and the more stridently as time goes on, and inevitably sometimes with every justification. Still, it is the case, and it will remain the case, that the universities service society with a steady and swelling stream of people trained to teach, to research, to build; to advise, to manage, to administer; to cure the body's ills (and, to a lesser extent, the mind's); to pronounce, to pontificate, to form opinion. Some say there are not enough of them; others that they are not good enough; and both are probably right. The social demand for graduates (i.e. skilled white-collar workers) has increased more rapidly than the output, and so is less than satisfied.[1] But the academic demand for excellence is as certainly unsatisfied, first by the slender element of general education built into most vocational and scientific courses, and second by the humdrum level and haphazard organization of the most highly favoured degree, the B.A.

Social demand is, then, being partially met. But social demand is capable of a different though related definition, which may be approached through a consideration of the function of the educational system as a whole. Like any other educational system it is supposed to improve the minds and increase the skills of those who pass through it, but the system itself and these specific results serve a further and more directly functional purpose. This may be indicated by saying that the total system is part of a greater social system which encourages a fair degree of social mobility. New Zealand is the sort of society which has social mobility (especially in an upward direction) built into it, and where, in any case, the range between top and bottom is not very great. It requires of an individual only a modicum of talent, energy and luck to move from the bottom to somewhere

[1] In 1959 the committee of inquiry chaired by Sir David Hughes Parry reported thus: 'It is clear that New Zealand requires urgently a substantial increase in the numbers of well-educated persons graduating from the universities, to meet both the present serious backlog and the increasing requirements of the professions, private industry and commerce, the educational institutions, and the public services in the years ahead' (*Report of the Committee on New Zealand Universities*, p. 22). This overall situation has not significantly altered in the last seven years.

A SOCIETY AND ITS UNIVERSITIES

near the top, for he does not have to go very far. Nor, in the case of an individual born at or near the top, is an absence of talent, energy and luck necessarily the cause of a considerable or abrupt downwards movement or even of a downward movement at all, for the strata are as persistent as mobility between them. But again, if the lack of these qualities does initiate a downward movement, the distance to be fallen is not great enough to cause undue catastrophe. All this is to suggest that New Zealand, while it is a society marked by upward mobility, is not a society further marked by the spectacular triumphs and catastrophic defeats which occur when this process is fierce and competitive. Mobility in New Zealand is certainly constant and pervasive, but it is also sluggish and co-operative. The educational system as a whole, including the universities, has participated (indeed, must participate) in this process.

They have turned (and they continue to turn) labourers' sons into outstanding lawyers, scientists, administrators and doctors. And at the same time they have turned professional men's sons into run-of-the-mill lawyers, scientists, etc. Thus they serve their necessary dual social role: upward mobility combined with the underpinning of established social position. This has certain consequences for university education: a wide-open entry system (school accrediting and provisional matriculation); facilities for part-time and external study; a second-chance examination system (special examinations, pass-as-a-whole devices, going through the same course again); a weak and nervously employed exclusion system; and a not too exacting graduation level. All this is necessary if, while the bright boy from the sticks flies through the system collecting honours as he goes, the less than bright boy from the expensive suburb can plod through to a social slot not too far removed from the conditions to which he has become accustomed.

There are some indications that, in recent years, stratification has hardened and mobility between the strata diminished. A prolonged labour shortage holds out high and immediate wage-prospects to the young worker, whether trained or not, thus reducing the incentive to acquire skills. So the narrow and short perspectives usual in a working-class home are not counteracted by economic incentives. The middle-class child, accustomed to wider and larger perspectives, and with an incentive to avoid low-status occupations, sets his foot upon the educational ladder with, in general, a much stronger motivation. Social background and individual motivation combine to preserve existing social distinctions, by minimizing incentive for the able working-class child and maximizing it for his middle-class intellectual equivalent. As a consequence, the larger towns are coming to know a hierarchy of secondary schools, ranging from technical schools in working-class suburbs, to the so-called 'academic' schools in the more expensive districts. (It would be surprising if in the single schools serving smaller towns, the children in the academic forms were not disproportionately drawn from middle-class homes, but this research has not been done.) The universities draw most of their students, and the abler of their students, from these middle-class academic schools, and so help to perpetuate social distinctions. There are sufficient exceptions to this process to make it still meaningful to talk about mobility. At present the universities seem poised between two social roles, and even-handedly both preserve and modify social stratification. But the continuance of present trends can only diminish their role as channels of mobility.

These social functions are seldom brought out in discussions on 'the university and society'. More often one hears (say) of the number of veterinarians predicted as necessary to service the livestock industry (and also the racehorse and the pet animal industries) ten years hence; the discussions would be nearer the heart of the matter if one heard, as well, of the number of young men and women who, to satisfy themselves socially, needed to become veterinarians. There is more than merely theoretical significance here. University planners assume (usually quite without empirical investigation) that, for example, the volume and value of exports will suffer if the appropriate graduate output falls below a certain level. The prediction may or may not be a correct one in a purely economic sense. but it may certainly be an insufficient one in a social sense. People become, let us say, engineers, for a host of reasons: perhaps because they wish to improve the efficiency of the economy, perhaps also because they like messing around with engines, or spending their working day in the open. It should not be assumed that because the narrow economic need for a certain skill is at a certain level, aspiration towards the personal satisfactions and social status accompanying the practice of that skill is at anywhere near the same level. A multitude of young men would seek to become, for example, farm advisers, doctors and lawyers in spite of a tapering off of the economic need for such specialists, should it ever occur.

In reverse, this situation has occurred in one field, in the education industry itself. The need for graduate secondary school teachers is fairly exactly predictable; as a result the administrators have induced and continue to induce a great number of impressionable and inexperienced school-leavers to accept a full-time university career with both a salary and a 'bond' i.e. a contractual obligation to teach. Many university teachers are keenly and unhappily aware of the reluctance of their final year students who now, less impressionable and more experienced, face and regret the future they had committed themselves to three or four years ago. It is not a matter of sympathizing so much with the graduates themselves as with their pupils when they are confronted by reluctant and even resentful teachers. Had those responsible for this bonded bursary scheme realized that school teaching is not regarded as a high-status occupation but indeed is placed quite low in the pecking order, they might have brought about, at the same time as they sent out the recruiting sergeants, an improvement of conditions within the profession, which would enable it to deliver more in the way of social satisfactions. Higher education is held in a web of very complex social demand, and its situation is not the more clearly understood if attention is paid only to the more readily measurable strands in the web.

It may be concluded from this analysis that the universities are profoundly influenced by social demand, both in its vocational and its more fundamental sociological aspects; that they are less sharply and fully aware of this situation than they could be expected to be; and that they should (if only to clear the ground for dissent and internal revolution) become more aware of the ways in which, socially, they resemble the church, the firm, the professional association, the trade union, the service club, the political party, and all other status-conferring social institutions. For dissent from and internal resistance to these time-honoured and ultimately unavoidable roles is a marked characteristic of the present-day universities.

II *The Internal Revolution*

To write of a revolution gives an impression of suddenness and completeness which the facts do not fully justify. Nevertheless, between the end of the Second World War and the present day a major change has occurred, and this change has arisen from a wider and deeper awareness by university teachers that they are members of an international profession with international standards and (this is the rub) an international pecking order. No one likes to be near the bottom of such an order or to be in danger of going there. The basic criticism levelled against the system from the earlier twentieth century had always been that New Zealand university education simply did not measure up to world standards; but the lot of those making this charge and trying to rectify the situation was frustration, or a job overseas, or piecemeal and isolated improvement within their own area of competence. The colleges were small and their rate of expansion slow: there were few opportunities for recruitment overseas and therefore little stimulus towards change.

The universities have responded to the expansion of the mid-century, perhaps somewhat tardily, but quite emphatically. Staff establishments have increased and new jobs have been filled, sometimes by promotion within the system but often by New Zealanders (and Australians) returning from postgraduate work overseas and by Britishers escaping from post-war austerity. Expansion has gone on to the present and, despite acute recruiting difficulties, continues. Between 1934 and 1964 the staff establishment increased sixfold (from 252 to 1,651), but the greater part of this expansion came late (in the late 1950s and in the 1960s) so that simultaneously staffs were trying to catch up, keep up and move ahead. Still, even by 1949 there were 536 university teachers at work, and this total included many whose experience of overseas universities had been both recent and formative.

The view that New Zealand university standards were too low was now held by a greater number of people, and the proportionate weight of those lulled into academic sleep was less. Further, to attract and hold staff, the universities set up refresher leave schemes, so that academics maintained contact with their subjects and their colleagues and could see their activities in a wide, challenging and sometimes humiliating context. The good men who had survived the lean years took fire; the new men, often at a sub-professorial level, kept the fires burning.

The result has been an across-the-board effort to raise standards, and this, in an open-entry system, has meant that the first year examinations have become a *de facto* entrance examination. (But, it must be added, a very inefficient one, for a unit system seldom sees a first year student failing all three or four of his units; more characteristically he gets one or two units, repeats his failed units the next year, and either retires from the race, or struggles through a degree which takes several years to complete.) Where two- and three-man departments once cut an entire discipline in halves or thirds, and necessarily taught in a generalized manner, now three, four or half-a-dozen actual or reputed specialists fasten upon a single course. If a student is taking three or four such courses in a year, he may find himself exhorted to greater and greater effort by a dozen or sixteen academics, people who at least skim through the journals, and sometimes people who actually read the books as well as the reviews. The sequel has not been unambiguously beneficial. Standards have certainly been raised, but haphazardly and at a price. The price has been the accentuation of the existing disjunctive features of the unit-system.

Even within a department there may not be very much co-ordination between the (perhaps) four people teaching a Stage I unit. Quite certainly there will (in arts and science faculties) be little or no co-ordination at all between the ten, twelve or more people teaching the three or four units making up a student's year's work. (This is not true of the new University of Waikato, where courses are organized in a co-ordinated manner, nor of the professional schools; but it is true of almost every other university faculty.) A very good student may well be able to cope with this invitation to schizophrenia; he may even, if he is quite exceptional, be able to co-ordinate the multitude of pressures into something that could be regarded as a year's work. If he does manage this he will have accomplished a quite heroic feat. But it is not at all certain that a university should require heroic virtue of its students, and it is quite certain that most students are incapable of it.

These remarks are particularly applicable to arts faculties (who teach nearly 40 per cent of all first degree students) and especially to first and second year work in such faculties. No arts students, in these years, will be specializing. Typically a good first year arts student will be simultaneously studying, say, English, history, philosophy and French in his first year, two of these subjects plus a fifth in his second, and two of the five in his third and final year. Even where honours first degrees in arts are provided (very recently in two of the six universities), he will not achieve specialization in one subject till his third year. More normally, specialization only comes in his postgraduate (fourth) year. In pure science the unit system still prevails, but its schizoid tendencies are limited by prescribed course-structures—e.g. a maths-physics specialization, or one in chemistry-biochemistry, or in the biological sciences. In the applied science and other vocational degree structures (e.g. law, commerce) the effect of the unit system is (in many cases) reduced by the orientation of all particular courses to a vocational goal, by the provision of specialist streams, and (sometimes) by an insistence on looking upon the year's work as a whole, and awarding passes and fails accordingly. All this is so; but still the problem of on-the-spot co-ordination remains: the student is still confronted with ten or a dozen bits in his year's work, and is not likely to find much evident co-ordination in the approaches of ten or a dozen lecturers. This means that arts lecturers could well pay attention to the aims (if not to the achievements) of their scientific and vocational colleagues. In one instance, as has been noted, they have done so: in the new University of Waikato arts courses are deliberately co-ordinated in a limited number of streams. So far the experiment is working with a very small roll: whether it will survive the separatist tendencies of specialists (disturbed because they cannot teach *enough* of their subjects) remains to be seen.

The picture in the arts faculties, and in the other faculties to some extent, is the consequence of specialization pressing for higher standards in an unco-ordinated manner. Though standards have been raised, an equally substantial academic problem remains, that of cohesion. Without doubt, a student in 'the bad old days', looked after by a small faculty of general practitioners, had a better prospect from this point of view. If he was lucky, and some were, he found himself advancing in a subject taught by a professor and a lecturer who knew the difference between generality and superficiality. He would absorb a smaller quantity of, say, history or mathematics or chemistry, but he could acquire a cultivated and engaged attitude to his subject, and so emerge as a better educated man than his equivalent of the 1960s. The graduate of the 1960s will probably have absorbed a greater quantity of his subject, but not necessarily in any co-ordinated manner, nor will he necessarily have acquired any cultivation or commitment from the battery of Ph.D.s to whose fire-power he has been subjected. He may even come to suspect that many of them have been firing blanks all the time. Indeed, if he (as a typical B.A. or B.Sc. student) takes four or five subjects in his degree, he will have listened to so many actual, potential or frustrated Ph.D.s that some of them are sure to have been firing blanks. But this is an occupational risk students run all over the world: can any university produce instances of worse lecturing, tutoring and supervision than Oxford or Cambridge? In New Zealand, especially in the arts faculties, but to some extent throughout the system, a further defect is added, the lack of co-ordination between the parts of a student's course, both within a single year, and between years. This defect is serious whether the lecturers are good, bad, or indifferent, and its removal would not require an improvement of the quality of the lecturing staff. The only thing that prevents it is the separateness of departments and the fatuity of faculties.

In the larger universities it is likely that departmental autonomy has gone so far that there is no cure possible within the structure of the general degree, and (as present honours degrees do not differentiate until the second or the third year) some considerable limit on the cure that may be effected there. This makes it likely that the only real cure is in the direction of radically increased subject specialization, so that a student will take a history degree or a philosophy degree (for example), as he cannot now. Departments, thus far, are small enough to be agents of co-ordination over a student's total course. It would be a pity, of course, to give up all ideas of a general education in arts or science; but it is hard to believe that the *status quo* is preferable.

The drive to raise academic standards has had, in this way, some regrettable consequences. It is a pity that the effort was made piecemeal, department by department. Surely it would not have been beyond the wit of administrators and teachers, in the early 1940s, to have recognized the consequences of the increasing secondary school rolls, and taken steps to co-ordinate courses and to direct entrants into them? The student population doubled in the 1940s (from just under 6,000 in 1939 to just over 12,000 in 1949); by the end of the decade the mere problem of passing vastly increased numbers through the same antiquated pipeline was sufficiently daunting. But in fact, not too many contrived to emerge at the further end. The following figures illustrate, first the sharp raising of the academic level, and second the wastage which occurs when the level is raised haphazardly and without effective thought about the human and social cost of such an action.

In 1951, 2,032 new students matriculated, there were 9,949 students attending lectures, and 991 completed bachelor's degrees. Five years later, in 1956, the figures for each groups were 2,284, 10,195, and 837. That over 2,000 entrants should, in five years, produce only a little over 800 graduates, is a disquieting statistic. The graduation rate has, in fact, remained remarkably stable, and has increased at a very much slower rate than the number of matriculants and the total size of the university population. Thus, in 1959, there were 3,804 new students commencing courses. In 1964, only 1,140 bachelor's degrees were completed. In 1965, over 6,000 first year students embarked upon their courses. It would be remarkable if many more than 1,500 graduates had emerged from this body by the end of this decade.[1] This damping down of the graduation rate is certainly a safeguard against academic inflation, but we may wonder if the penal consequences of such a laudable intention need have been so great. No one, it is sure, could confidently assert that about three-quarters of entrants are,

---

[1] The figures given in this paragraph are generally, rather than precisely, reliable. As some students take many more than five years to complete what is nominally a three year degree course, any year's graduation figure will contain students who began work anything from three years to half a lifetime before. But such lengthy undergraduate periods are in themselves a wastage, and the existence of such graduates would in fact reduce the number graduating within five years.

in the nature of things, hopeless, even in an open-entry university system. If a university in New Zealand was not, for most students, the sort of intellectually bewildering environment which it has become, the wastage would not be so great, and standards could remain intact.

However, the rate of graduation is not the whole story. The assumption which government departments, business organizations and university administrators agree to make is that social need is to be measured in terms of graduate output. The teacher, for his part, is often aware that the gap between the person who, for any one of a multitude of extra-academic reasons, fails to graduate, and the person who, for any one of a multitude of equally extra-academic reasons, manages to graduate, is at the very least not wide, often non-existent, and not too infrequently a gap which does credit to the non-graduate. He may look a little cynically at the status and emolument awarded to the man who has bull-dozed or tricked his way into a 'C minus' degree. But planners must measure, and their unit of measurement must in this context be the graduate. This will do no great harm, as long as the planners realize that when they are able to say that 360 university-trained persons are being injected into the public service, they have perhaps not said a great deal; for many of the graduates will not make much, if any, difference, being, at best, merely efficient oilers and greasers of the institutional machine. The quality of graduates, in the view of the teacher, could always be higher; but, thanks to the appreciating level of social demand, it will never be very much higher.

Most of the teachers, and at least some of the planners, will have one eye on that range of achievement which stretches up like Jacob's ladder from 'C minus' to 'A double plus'. Here the teacher may dissent from the convenient assumption, and assert that the scholarly value of his work is to be judged by the quality of the people he sends out with top honours, and the true social value of his work by the people he sends out with more moderate distinctions. The assertion will not carry much conviction to those who have little experience of what is being asserted, for excellence is notoriously resistent to quantification. In the end pretty well everyone falls back upon riding his hunch. But, demonstrable or not, it is surely not unreasonable to suggest that the community is well served by scholars who lead in their disciplines, and by graduates who devote sometimes unqualified brilliance, and more often very notable competence and insight, to such fields as administration, applied research, teaching or (in the case of most women graduates) motherhood. Proof may elude him, but if the teacher after some years behind the lectern can look around him and see, of his former pupils, a small handful in high academic positions at home and overseas, and a more numerous group at work as more than usually efficient teachers, administrators, research workers, clergymen and community leaders, he may conclude that he and the system have not done too badly by society, even if the education industry is still short on its annual graduate quota.

Here, indeed, there is some room for comfort. The level of the bachelor's degree had too far to climb for its present standing to be noteworthy; but the level of the top graduates —honours' bachelors, masters and doctors—has been good and seems to have become better. At the upper levels of a student's course, when he has survived the bewilderment of his initiation, the more specialized nature of contemporary teaching comes into its own. The student who has survived his early years is, by definition, either very discerning or very unfeeling; the former sort may be expected to grow under the teacher's eyes as he finishes his first degree and goes on to postgraduate work. A New Zealand graduate with good honours may still, especially in the arts, be short on specialization; but he will have gone fairly deeply into one discipline and be ready to go confidently out of his depth. Often, to do so, he will either need or want to go overseas, and too often for the country's and the universities' good, he will stay there. But that is the dilemma of any provincial society; it may be regretted, but there is no prospect of it being avoided.

III   *Poverty in the Midst of Plenty*

The best thing about James McGill, according to Stephen Leacock, is that he is dead. The worst thing about New Zealand's James McGills is that they have not been born. There may be a few millionaires in the country, but if so they keep very quiet, and they certainly do not endow universities.[1] It is not an easy country in which to amass a great fortune; its resources are limited in number and quality and its domestic market is small. It lives on its grasslands, the products of which it exports overseas, and this activity has built up a large number of modest futures rather than a small number of large ones. It has not the base, either in raw materials or (at present) in special skills, for an industrial economy. All economic activity is restricted by high labour costs, by the high cost of imported raw materials and equipment, and by the distance or the smallness of markets.

Private endowment, then, is an entirely insignificant part of university finance. So is the smaller-scale benevolence from alumni and well-wishers which counts for so much in the United Kingdom and North America. The tax structure bears heavily on individuals (who may reach the maximum rate of 13/6 in the pound at £3,600) and upon companies; further, neither individuals nor companies may claim tax exemption for substantial gifts to, for example, universities.[2] Just because nearly everyone pays tax, nearly everyone concludes that he has done his bit for his country in doing so. The government is left paying all the bills; and it must be said at the outset that government has, over recent years, paid some heavy educational bills and has committed itself to some heavy ones in the future.

Nor, to continue to list misfortunes, do New Zealand

---

[1] The University of Canterbury, as an exception, recently received a substantial legacy from a New Zealand-born Australian, but the occurrence is isolated enough to be newsworthy.

[2] A recent change enables companies to claim exemption on amounts up to £500 donated to research. Individuals may claim exemption on amounts up to £25 for sums donated for purposes which include education.

universities have the advantage of a federal political system, in which (as in Australia) federal initiative has stimulated state governments out of their traditional parsimony. Finally, it must be mentioned that though in the later nineteenth century some attempts were made to endow the new colleges with land, this was not on a scale sufficient to mean anything for the future. The universities have a single paymaster,[1] and it speaks volumes for the fair-mindedness of successive governments that they have seldom attempted to call the tune. The universities have been left to do what they judge best with the money they have been given. External influence upon the universities is great, but it is exercised constitutionally—e.g., through considerable lay representation on governing bodies; through the Education Department and professional bodies having a voice on matters of curricula; through Treasury making its representations on salary deliberations. It may be over-great, but it is neither covert nor crippling; the universities hire (but never fire), teach, and research in sufficient freedom.[2] If there are major limits on this freedom, they are self-imposed, as administrators, aware of their dependence, ask themselves what governments want and what they will put up with.

Over the last twenty years government spending on university education, and upon education generally, has increased considerably. Had the universities been even moderately well-equipped in 1945, then spending at the subsequent level would have been almost all one could have wished for. But, if they had not been so deplorably under-equipped in 1945, subsequent spending would not have been at this level, and today we would be in much the same position. A good deal of money was imperatively needed to

[1] Doubly a single paymaster, for that considerable part of annual income which is represented by students' fees comes chiefly from state-provided students' bursaries.

[2] From time to time a politician may be found assailing, usually in conditions of privilege, the political reliability of named university teachers. Of recent years a Cabinet minister, Mr. T. P. Shand, has distinguished himself in this manner.

catch up on the arrears accruing from previous decades of neglect. This, however, was the very period in which the universities were faced with a need to *expand* in response to the social and academic demands described earlier. Roughly, the amount of money spent since 1945 would have been sufficient *either* for catching-up *or* for expansion. It has not been adequate for these two needs operating simultaneously.[1]

At the end of the war the universities were inadequate from almost very point of view. Primitive and overcrowded buildings, which had hardly been added to since the early twentieth century, were quickly surrounded by penumbras of wartime prefabs, many of which are still in use, now overcrowded in their turn (they were always primitive). Hostels, both university and privately owned, housed a small proportion of the student population, and this situation continues in spite of some subsequent additions. Libraries were very poorly supplied both with books and places for readers. Today only three of the universities have new library buildings, and though holdings have grown, so has student and staff demand, probably more rapidly. Laboratories were small, cramped, under-financed and poorly equipped; again improvements (new buildings in many cases, new equipment in all) have not kept pace with staff or student numbers, nor, and this is especially im-

---

[1] That government spending on university education has increased both considerably and belatedly may be seen from the following table (figures are in £m).

	1934	1939	1944	1949	1954	1959	1964
	−5	−40	−5	−50	−5	−60	−5
Current expenditure	·06	·16	·21	·78	1·48	2·21	5·57
Buildings etc.	−	·02	·05	·27	·23	·98	3·10

These figures should be set beside the increase in enrolment:

1934	1939	1944	1949	1954	1959	1964
4,721	5,979	7,730	12,030	11,510	14,891	20,262

In brief, the warning of the 1940s was not heeded until the 1960s. It was not heeded as emphatically as these figures would suggest, for inflation over the whole of the period covered has affected costs of all kinds.

portant, with the research needs of staff and postgraduate students. This last applies to libraries regarded as the laboratory-equivalent for research in the humanities: no university library is a research library except in a spasmodic way. Thanks to, perhaps, the persuasiveness of a particular staff-member, coverage over a limited area might be quite good, but of the next-related area almost non-existent. In laboratories and libraries alike, each university must choose between undergraduate needs and research needs; typically an attempt is made to do both at once, so that neither is well done.

Again, at the end of the war, the staffing establishment was quite inadequate. Here one is tempted to complain that in spite of an improvement in ratios since, these ratios are still some distance behind the better United Kingdom, United States and Australian examples. But another and much more important circumstance enters here: every university has a number of positions which it either cannot fill, or can only fill after long delays. Inadequate as present ratios may be, if the universities could readily fill every post which the ratios enable them to create, they would not be worrying unduly about the ratios. Here a further financial consideration enters—staff salaries—not in isolation, but rather in relation to the other inadequacies just mentioned.

Staff salaries have risen considerably—the pre-war professor earned about as much as the recently graduated junior lecturer today. However, the cost of living has hardly stood still over the interval. At the present a professor's salary compares quite well, inside New Zealand, with top salaries in government and business, but not too well with self-employed professional and business men. By and large, the university teacher has achieved a reasonable position within the New Zealand salary structure. But university teaching and research is an international profession, and parity outside the country is more important from a re-cruiting point of view than parity inside. At the moment, this parity does not exist, either with the U.K., from which New Zealand traditionally recruits staff, or with Australia, its traditional recruiting rival. Nor, because many New Zealanders go for postgraduate training overseas and because Australian universities advertise in New Zealand papers, can the universities be at all confident of holding their own abler products. It is a real danger that the universities will, before long, have on their staffs too high a proportion of those who are there simply because they are unemployable elsewhere. A leaven of patriots would remain, but the lump would be very heavy.

It does not seem that this salary disadvantage can be permanently removed. New Zealand increases are quickly cancelled out by new British and Australian increases. Typically, New Zealand inches towards parity with Australia as Australia more expeditiously prepares to reach a new standard. Short of the sort of increase which would put New Zealand professors on internal parity with the most well-to-do business and professional men, this is a race which New Zealand is doomed to be forever losing.[1] This is probably appreciated by governments and may account, more than parsimony or ignorance, for their reluctance to accept or apply the principle of parity with overseas countries.

Still, money may do other things than raise salaries. Already, an appreciable difference has been made to research by the larger sums distributed by the Research Grants Committee and by the controllers of a share of state lottery profits. This has gone chiefly into expensive scientific equipment, though smaller but still useful sums have greatly assisted non-experimental research: £500 will buy an historian a decent amount of microfilm. If, both centrally and in each university, a good deal more money could be

[1] A substantial increase came into effect on 1 January 1964. In an article published in September 1965, Professor F. W. Holmes reported: 'Of the 152 positions [since] advertised, 44 per cent have not been filled; 30 per cent of the 23 chairs advertised, 60 per cent of the 51 senior lectureships and 48 per cent of the 97 lectureships have remained vacant' (*N.Z. Journal of Public Administration*, 28. 1, p. 11). The more moderate increase due to come into effect in 1967 seems unlikely to alter this situation.

found to finance research, and also to build up libraries to a research standard on a broad front, this would create job satisfactions which would offset a moderate salary lag. But the salary lag, while it may be inevitable, must only be moderate, and it must be kept moderate with swift rather than laggardly adjustments. For, be an academic as well-equipped for research as he could possibly hope for, he will not be able to do very much if he is forever teaching. Staffing ends, as it begins, with ratios, and salaries to fill the jobs the ratios create.

Laggardness operates in another way to depress the university situation. Each institution operates upon a quinquennial grant. About all that one can say with real confidence about a five-year period is that expansion will go on within it. How much expansion—given the immediacy with which social demand is conveyed to the universities and the alacrity of their response, chiefly for open-entry but also for new courses—is beyond the skill of planners to predict. In most institutions, rolls are running ahead, sometimes well ahead, of predictions made at the beginning of the present quinquennium. The consequent inelasticity is crippling: nearly everyone is getting by on less money than they actually need, and less, too, than they could, some years previously, have reasonably foreseen that they would need had they foreseen the demand. Greater elasticity is necessary, either by shortening the period, or by providing for additional grants to cope with the unpredictable.

In all this, the universities (unless they should choose to adopt such coercive techniques as restriction of entry or deliberate overspending) are very much at the mercy of the University Grants Committee, and especially of its Chairman. This co-ordinating and supervising body is the very lively ghost of the old federal University of New Zealand.[1]

[1] The four older universities completed their progress towards full autonomy in 1961 with the abolition of the University of New Zealand. The two new universities (Massey at Palmerston North and Waikato at Hamilton) came into existence with full autonomy in 1964. The former took its chief origin from an agricultural college set up in 1926.

In particular, the U.G.C. is responsible for negotiation with government on all matters of finance, chiefly salary scales, building programmes, research grants and the quinquennial block grants for each university, together with their break-down into five yearly sums. The separate universities play a fairly passive part in all this. In preparation for each quinquennium, they tell the U.G.C. what they want to do and how much they will need to do it. In reply, and after negotiations to which the universities are not privy, the U.G.C. tells each university how much each will have, but not what it shall do with it. The next five years show how well or ill the guessers guessed.

Under its first chairman, Dr. F. J. Llewellyn, the U.G.C. had notable success in getting government approval in principle to a substantial building programme, though this does not take away the government's ability to reduce, postpone, or even refuse, expenditure on any particular item when it comes up. On other matters, Dr. Llewellyn's period was less glorious. On salary scales and quinquennial grants it is widely regarded as a partial failure: widely, though perhaps ignorantly, for no one can say whether or not, in negotiations in which the universities as such did not take part, Dr. Llewellyn took the government as far as it was, under pressure, prepared to go.

This argument has had a constantly plaintive note. Why, when one writes of the universities of a country having a high standard of living, should this be so? First, because university education is very, and increasingly, expensive; second, because, though the people live well, the country is not unambiguously rich; and thirdly, because New Zealand governments have a great number of demands made upon them, and long ago the overmastering choice was made for welfare.

It has already been suggested that among the early forma-tive influences upon the university system was an equali-tarian ethos not especially tolerant of excellence. This may be less so today than then, but it is still sufficiently potent to raise an initial prejudice against the idea that a very great amount of public money should be spent to produce an excellent university structure. Such excellence would not be condemned out of hand, but its expense could lead to the conclusion that it could be done without.

Again, it has been said that New Zealand's wealth is of a patchy and precarious kind. It is not conducive to large scale capital accumulation, and does not produce the surplus which Renaissance princes or American millionaires could be persuaded to invest in culture. The state, for its part, collects a considerable revenue, but since the war it has been constantly obliged to damp down inflationary tendencies, and so to limit its own spending, especially on capital works. But more, the state, since the later nineteenth century, has been sensitive to an ever-expanding range of social service and welfare demands; from a government point of view spending on education is simply one aspect of spending on social services. There are many others, of equal or greater priority, and any government will feel obliged to keep them in equilibrium. This obligation precludes a level of spending on education which would threaten the claims of, for example, social security benefits. Disgruntled academics often look at the steadily increasing expenditure on defence and reflect how much better off the country would be if only it didn't throw money down that sort of drain but instead diverted it to education. Across the Tasman, Australian defence spending is at a much higher level, and so is government spending on university education. But Australian governments devote a much smaller share of their resources to social welfare. In New Zealand the pensioner has as good a claim as the soldier to be regarded as the universities' chief handicap.

One quite basic situation has been ignored so far. It is that New Zealand has chosen to provide six universities for a little over $2\frac{1}{2}$ million people. Given the absence of other sources of money, given the pressures which will prevent any major disproportion in the share-out between the six, and given the likelihood that overall spending will remain at a fairly low level, it does not seem unreasonable to conclude that $2\frac{1}{2}$ million people will not be able to support six universities of the highest standard. Nor is it likely that one or two will become favoured children and the rest relatively neglected. We will have six universities which, from some points of view, will be modest, not to say mediocre, institutions. Yet this, as the last section of this essay will argue, does not mean that they will be unable to develop their characteristic qualities, and even some areas of excellence. But such an achievement must be preceded by an acknowledgment of severe limitations, and it will not be produced by a constant mourning for an unattainable ideal.

IV   *The Ideological Imperative*

If one could choose for a country a set of origins and continuing influences, one would not, without hesitation, settle for a combination which included an early Victorian birthday, a preponderantly British and Protestant early-industrial ancestry, a small population, a lop-sided economy, a provincial and homogeneous society, a narrow and restrictive ideology, a derivative value-system, a dependent national character, an absence of self-reliance. One would not opt for quite so much Britishness, nor Britishness of quite that variety. Such characteristics preclude so much that one may not, without an element of dehumanization, deplore: Latin grace and German seriousness, urban variety and rural solidity, intellectual conservatism and rational radicalism, a capacity to stand fast and a readiness to take risks. Instead, there will be much that, if there is too much of it, one may only deplore: Anglo-Saxon stodge and hypocrisy, urbanization without urbanity, a peasantry without continuity, conservatism without ideas and radicalism without purpose, a permanent hesitation between what one has and what one would like to have. This of course is a caricature, but a caricature may be in order. A country which has so regularly failed to accept history's invitations to draw its own portrait must be depicted either with extreme hesitation, or in a way which seeks to emphasize by distortion. And, from the humbug of the early settlers setting up antipodean Etons, to the vanity of politicians begging for Royal Tours (the most recent by an American President) the invitations have been declined—in so far as they have been recognized.

To an extent these invitations have been accepted by some people, but by painters, novelists and poets more emphatically than by academics, though some have doubled the roles. If there is some hesitancy in the acceptance and some lack of definition in the resulting statements, if there is an almost total lack of stridency and even of vehemence, this points to a persistent wavering of confidence; not a constant failure of nerve but a constant fear that nerve would fail. And this, in its turn, stems from still dominant conditions of origin and growth, and the absence of more recent developments able to counteract them. In Australia major industrial resources have been exploited, large-scale immigration has altered the character of the people; the future cuts the past down to size. None of these things, or their equivalents, has happened *in* New Zealand. On the contrary, the changes that have taken place have happened *to* New Zealand: the diminution of British power, the precariousness of the British market, the shift in the balance of power in the Pacific region. New Zealand has been acted upon; it has not tried to take its destiny in its own hands. Dependence has deepened as its nature has altered. The inherited attitudes of dependence and provincialism have reluctantly and fearfully (but seldom, alas, resentfully) altered their focus, not their nature. In New Zealand the past always cuts the future down to size.

This is to write of pervasive social attitudes, not of the initiatives of individuals. There have been such initiatives, and they have made some impact upon the ethos of the universities. They have not been as considerable as they might have been, and they have followed external pressures and never anticipated them. But it is something that there have been any, even if it must be conceded at the outset that in the universities they have been less emphatic than the responses of a handful of writers, painters and musicians.

The universities, in part by becoming places in which people write and paint and compose,[1] and in part by providing a running commentary upon the work of artists, should share with the country's creative individuals the task of taking the first steps towards a national life as self-determined as a country may be in the mid-twentieth century. Even for great powers the scope for self-determination is not wide; for small powers it is narrow to the point of exigence. But this very narrowness makes it all the more imperative that even a small opportunity should be accepted. In their acceptance of this opportunity lies the utility of those university teachers whose cause may not be pleaded in terms of social and economic efficiency. They are concerned with the social goals proposed and made possible by mere efficiency—they make little direct impact upon (for example) the growth-rate of the economy, but they may, and should, do two equally useful jobs. They should, first, keep it in the public mind that economic growth is not a self-authenticating activity, but a pointless one unless it has a supra-economic purpose; and they should, second, share in the process by which that purpose is defined and kept in a state of constant re-definition. These objectives, rather than the sort of hobbyism which too often characterizes their teaching and research, should be the professional concern of scholars in the social sciences and humanities.

They should, briefly, be concerned to explore, clarify and, in a marginal way, create the identity of their society. Within any view of society less restrictive than the ant-hill model, they will then serve as utilitarian a role as the engineer and the accountant. This is not to say that utility should be their direct goal—just as scientists should not be limited to short-term technological objectives. It is to say, simply, that they should be alive to the social applications

[1] Only the University of Otago, through two fellowships, makes provision for creative work as a formal aspect of the life of the university, though many writers and other artists are employed as teachers by the universities.

of their work, and that, as academics in search of the status, rewards and satisfactions which even a humble university confers, they should be constantly at work on the business of application. It is to say that remoteness and hobbyism should be excluded from their professional lives.

The purpose of these paragraphs is to suggest for arts teachers (the largest single group of academics in New Zealand) a valid social role which is also a valid intellectual activity. Scientists and technologists, perhaps, have no need to worry, for even if they are not really as socially useful as they are reputed to be, nevertheless they are underwritten by a socio-academic mystique which spares them both the pains and benefits of introspection. Arts teachers caught between the effortless security of their scientific colleagues and the knowledge that the really momentous work in their fields goes on at Harvard and Oxford, need to worry more about their relevance. Here it is argued that they may find it, in New Zealand, in an activity which is aimed at maximizing the community's awareness of itself, at deepening and re-fining its sense of identity, and thereby at giving it a capacity for self-determination in a world little receptive to this goal. They may do so by accepting the ideological imperative of history and locality, by discovering the country in which they, by choice, habit, or necessity, live. Some predictable consequences would proceed from the acceptance of this imperative: a reshaping of the overall pattern of their work, intensifying what is there only marginally at present, off-loading what is there merely because previous models have been uncritically accepted. The new model, projecting a different pattern, can be sketched out in three divisions: tradition, locality, and region. Too much in New Zealand university education, especially in the arts, is the continuing result of the sort of timidity and nervelessness already discussed; too little has arisen from a readiness to experiment even at the risk of running off the rails. A tradition is something to examine and establish, not to accept listlessly; a locality is a place for a whole life, not for a partial exile; a region needs to be inhabited, not patronized out of relevance. All three have to be lived in, not merely lived with.

The transmission of a tradition is the special, though neither the exclusive nor the sole, function of the humanities. It will not cease to be the case that New Zealanders think and behave in ways which they share with Europeans generally. It would, as a consequence, be a mutilation to exclude Aristotle, Chaucer, Molière, Marx and Joyce from the programme. The danger, in effect, is rather the reverse; that they will exclude everyone and everything else, and exclude most notably the points at which they impinge upon the New Zealand in which the student lives, its character, its ethics, its literature and its politics. The job of the humanities is indeed to transmit and to transform, not merely to venerate; to make connections, not merely to examine one of the poles which are available for connecting up.

The locality in which the tradition makes its impact is, creatively, very much the field of the humanities, but the direct work of exploring it is in a special sense the task of history and the social sciences. Ideally a university should subject its society to the scrutiny of literary and art critics, historians, economists, sociologists, anthropologists, and political scientists, and should provide, both in its research activity and in its teaching programmes, a point at which the insights of all may cohere. Such locality studies, to be fruitful, need to be comparative, and some of the comparisons can well occur within the country's broader region —in New Zealand's case, the Pacific and its surrounding countries. From this region, further, constantly arise influences which modify the inherited tradition. Throughout her history New Zealand has been influenced not merely by the European tradition direct, but also by this tradition as mediated through North American and Australian experience. Influences from the Pacific region are increasing in the later twentieth century. Hence they require study not simply as part of the country's broader region, but as an element in the country's tradition. As yet Japan, China and India have had little impact upon New Zealand, and Latin

America none at all. Such a state of affairs can hardly continue, especially as the New Zealand economy, to stay healthy, will need to find markets in this Pacific region. Here the universities should anticipate the likely connections and modifying influences, so that the country could be ready to absorb influences critically and selectively rather than passively.

New Zealand, more than most countries, is wide open to outside influences, and its only way to prevent cultural obliteration is to be aware of what is going on, to select and reject in accord with a sense of national identity, to internalize the influences which cannot be avoided. This requires, above all else, an awareness of what it is that people call New Zealand, and a sense of deep identity with it. Perhaps it is essentially through the creative arts that a country shapes and recognizes its own image; but in their more pedestrian way, researchers and teachers may play their part, by ordering and transmitting the insights of the artists, and through their own special understanding. The supreme need in the humanities and social sciences in New Zealand universities is for an attention to New Zealand character and structure as useful, as direct, and as detailed, as the attention paid by scientists to New Zealand soils, crops and animals.

A good deal of work of this kind is in fact going on in the universities: the remarkable thing is that it has been so recently begun, and that it represents so small a proportion of the universities' overall effort. There has been a fair output of research in New Zealand history and economics (but, strangely, too little of a specialized kind in economic history), politics, anthropology and ethnography. Yet one must itemize some notable lacks. There is a deplorable poverty in sociology; a paucity of research on the Maori situation since European contact (cf. the relative wealth on Polynesian archaeology and anthropology); and little of significance in political sociology, e.g. interest group studies. Literature is served by a handful of general works and a handful of specialist articles; but there is only one biographical study of an important literary figure (nor, for that matter, are there more than four decent biographies of New Zealand politicians). The plastic arts are largely, and music almost entirely, unstudied. No church, trade union, professional group, and only one political party, has been the subject of a thorough published study. No social history of any rigour exists: is it significant that the best historical talent in New Zealand has been devoted to the process of discovery, racial conflict, external relations, and a few notable expatriates? There are, indeed, a multitude of local and regional histories, but those of significant quality could be counted on the fingers of one hand. No reasonable history exists of the two largest cities. Nor has any single industry been scrutinized as a whole and over the full period of its development. There is very much more to be done than has been done, and if the universities do not do it, it is hard to see who will.

One consequence should be the development of postgraduate research in the humanities and social sciences. Each year only a handful of Ph.D.s are completed in departments connected with literature, language, history and the social sciences, and many of these are the work of relatively senior staff members, not of regular full-time postgraduate students. Only a moderate spending on fellowships, library resources and equipment would be necessary to get a true postgraduate programme off the ground in the six universities. A further step is often advocated: that New Zealand should set up a National University devoted to research, and risk the possibility that such a university would cream off a good deal of the talent in existing universities. If such a National University were well financed and carefully planned around those activities in which New Zealand offers unusual opportunities for research, the risk would be worth running, and the long-term result would be to feed back talent into the teaching universities.

In some areas of the social sciences, New Zealand does possess quite unique opportunities—for example, in anthropology, sociology, politics, and economics, and in history in so far as historians are prepared to serve under these banners. The Maori element in the New Zealand population, its pre-European culture, its experience of culture change, and its adaptations to the dominant European culture, together with the energy and intelligence with which the Maoris have responded to their transformation, present opportunities to the ethnologist, archeologist, anthropologist and sociologist. Only a beginning has been made on studies in this area, and the university contribution to the considerable body of information that exists is not greater than that made by other institutions and by freelance scholars. The one notable cultural anthropologist who was of Maori race, Sir Peter Buck, emerged in the 1920s and found scope for his talents, not in a New Zealand university, but at Yale and at the Bishop Museum at Honolulu. In forty years a good deal has changed for the better: departments of anthropology at Auckland and Otago and of psychology at Wellington have been distinctly productive, and new departments at Wellington and Waikato promise well. But it still remains to be noted that one of the minute band of scholars of Maori race is doing research in twentieth century Maori history at the Australian National University.

More generally, New Zealand society as a whole is a fair field for the social scientist. It is small, it has one major and several minor racial minorities, it is both isolated and permanently influenced from outside, it is both fluid and stratified, its political processes are both intricate and accessible, it is highly urbanized and basically rural, its past and its present are reflected in an abundance of statistics. It is large enough to contain variety and small enough to be looked at as a whole. It is a natural sample awaiting more rigorous and prolonged attention than researchers have yet been able to devote to it. Research of this kind is not unduly expensive. Either good research schools in the existing universities, or a National University, or both, could move in on this field in a more emphatic and thorough way than has yet been the case, for the cost of a single cyclotron. And the opportunities, if they were backed up by appropriate salaries and facilities, could draw scholars to New Zealand.

The benefit would be shared by the society and by scholarship itself.

If it may be assumed that university education in New Zealand is not going to be financed on a lavish scale, then certain types of scientific research—e.g. in nuclear physics —should be automatically excluded from such a programme. Nor is it easy to see why the country should invest in a shoestring duplication of research which will be conducted under much more favourable circumstances elsewhere in the world. But problems which arise naturally from the country's social and economic life suggest a less expensive and more rewarding area for concentrated investigation. To a considerable extent this work is being done in the existing universities and research institutes. However, none of them would agree that it was being done on a large enough scale. Here again, moderate expenditure would maximize research output, and do good equally to society and scholarship. Again, a National University could lead, stimulate and supply the existing institutions and draw to the country overseas scholars.

Postgraduate schools organized around such interests would have a regional rather than a merely local reference. Polynesian studies generally should find their proper world centre in New Zealand, and New Zealand should be as well known for its anthropologists as it is for its footballers. Many problems in race relations—the assimilation of ethnic minorities, the urbanizing of rural groups, the role of government as an agent in culture change—exist throughout the Asian and Pacific region on a vast scale: in New Zealand they exist on a small scale and so are the more readily available for close study. Certain technologies, especially those connected with dairy production and soils, have been taken to an advanced stage in New Zealand, and are vital to economic and social development in Asia and the Pacific. Already, chiefly through the Colombo Plan, New Zealand experience and skill has been transferred to South East Asia. Though on a much smaller scale, the economic problems of the Pacific islands are acute and likely to benefit from a similar transfer. Here, proportionately, New Zealand assistance equivalent in volume to that given to South East Asia under the Colombo Plan, could benefit the total life of small island communities. More broadly, the Pacific islands, to many of which New Zealand is connected by an Imperial (and a New Zealand sub-imperial) past, need teachers, administrators, specialists of all kinds, and simply a higher level of mass education. New Zealand's present contribution to the educational needs of this area is inconsiderable in relation to the size of the problem.

A significant part of the research undertaken in New Zealand universities should follow the directions set by the country's history and likely future development into the Pacific region. This would mean, from one point of view, that the country was accepting something of an elder brother role, with all its dangers. But, from another and a counter-vailing point of view, the role would be self-interested and self-validating. It would be based upon New Zealand's vulnerability to disturbances and animosities arising in this region; on New Zealand's inevitably close relationship with the peoples of this area; and upon the country's need to know, rather more than to help, the countries and peoples it must grow with if it is to grow at all. That is to say, a concern with locality involves a concern with region. And a concern with both, moreover, involves a concern with tradition, under two aspects—as the chiefly West European tradition which New Zealand, among other countries, has localized in this region; and as the decreasingly West European tradition which the locality and the region progressively transform.

All this amounts to a suggestion that in New Zealand's universities resources should be directed to activities where the return will be greatest. The universities should develop their strengths, not deplore their weaknesses. These potential strengths include those areas of activity, in the arts and in the sciences, where social utility may be most fruitfully served. The universities and their society would still be in a relation of tension, but of tension within an overall identity. It is easier to see how such an orientation should shape the research activity of a university than to prescribe the ways in which it should re-shape teaching. But the former should guide and indeed create the latter; and if it could be set along the proper course the rest would—haphazardly no doubt—follow. In no sense would the whole programme be irrelevant to the needs of New Zealand society; neither would it be other than exacting and professional, nor would it prove too forbiddingly expensive.

Index